Julia Solis

# New York Underground
## The Anatomy of a City

**Routledge** New York • London

Published in 2005 by
Routledge
270 Madison Ave
New York, NY 10016
www.routledge-ny.com

Published in Great Britain by
Routledge
2 Park Square
Milton Park, Abingdon
Oxon OX14 4RN
www.routledge.co.uk

Originally published in German as New York Underground: Anatomie einer Stadt
©Christoph Links Verlag—LinksDruck GmbH, Berlin 2002

Routledge is an imprint of the Taylor & Francis Group.

Printed in the United States of America on acid-free paper.

Typesetting: Jack Donner, BookType

10 9 8 7 6 5 4 3 2

Library of Congress Cataloging-in-Publication Data

Solis, Julia.
    [New York Underground. English]
    New York Underground: The Anatomy of a City / by Julia Solis ; translated by Julia Solis.
    p. cm.

    Originally published in German as New York Underground : Anatomie einer Stadt—T.p. verso.
    Includes bibliographical references and index.
    ISBN 0–415–95013–9 (hb: alk. paper)
    1. Underground areas—New York (State)—New York—Guidebooks. 2. New York (N.Y.)—
Guidebooks. I. Title.
    F128.18.S65 2004
    917.47'10443—dc22
                                                              2004009987

This book is dedicated to the Croton Maid

# Contents

# Acknowledgments

My foremost thanks to Revs for keeping me anchored to the ground. Thanks to you I just keep getting dirtier.

This book would not have been written without the influence of the infernal John Law, who has provided endless inspiration and prodding. I am humbly grateful to John and my other cohorts for sticking with me in the underground: the always debonair Chris Beauchamp, who introduced me to the Croton Aqueduct; Chris Hackett, who introduced me to the word "superdangerous"; Aaron Benoy, Mike Whalen, and Gary Burns for being the bomb all around; Bryan Papciak and Jeff Sias for their brilliance in the darkest places; Harry Haller and Rob Schmitt for chair-hopping through the skankiest waters; Joe Anastasio for derailing me with foamer speak; Steve Duncan, Andy Hogger, Nick, and Hilary for inviting me to play in their backyards.

A shout-out goes to my collaborators in all manners of subterranean activities, especially Anne Polster, Jason Cruz, Jeff Stark, Maureen Flaherty, Gayle Snible, Francine Rosado, Hans-Christoph Steiner, Christos Pathiakis, Scott Beale, and Ryan O'Connor, to name only a few. I'm also very grateful to all those who have shared research and experiences, particularly Theodore Grunewald, Roger Smith, Sheldon Lustig, Peter Dougherty, and Joe Schipani.

For their generosity in providing material and access to some of the sites mentioned here, I'm much indebted to Conrad Milster, George Tamaro Jr., Father Thomas Kallumady, Robert Lobenstein, Carl Vincent, Terry Kennedy, Carl Mehling, Frank da Cruz, Kevin Walsh, Diana Biederman, Harry Hassler, and Creative Time. A special thanks to David McBride, Robert Tempio, Riky Stock, Nicola Scott, Jeff Hall, and the New York Foundation for the Arts for their help in getting this edition published. And lastly, thanks to Bob Diamond for giving me a copy of the Viele map, which will never cease to enthrall me.

# New York Underground

*Figure 1.1  Inside the Croton Aqueduct*

CHAPTER ONE

# Introduction

New Yorkers have long been fascinated by the underground. Even a century ago, New York was described as a city of cave dwellers, whose cellars had many levels and whose communal Main Street had been superseded by the subway, with stations serving as new market squares. From labyrinthine diagrams, urban legends, and reports from the trenches, it would seem that if New York's underground were uncovered, a maze of canyons and chasms, riddled with a dense network of conduits and tunnels, would meet our eyes. The city's history is filled with attempts to harness the world below its streets. Possessing the world's most formidable collection of skyscrapers nicely shows how well New York stands up to engineering challenges. But at least a few New Yorkers know that the real adventure is far below, down the elevator shaft with the sandhogs, where you can feel and smell what New York is really made of and where the very fabric of the city vibrates with life.

Exploring New York's underground brings many surprises. One is that the hidden areas beneath the streets can be strangely peaceful and welcoming. It is specifically in its subterranean realms that this often chaotic metropolis becomes approachable; the secret spaces of the underground, desolate and beautiful, are the intimate surfaces of this gargantuan city. Above ground, New York treats its abandoned structures like seeds stuck between its teeth; well-meaning forces jab at them, hoping to reintegrate them into usefulness, yet eventually they are crushed or absorbed. In losing its ruins, the city is giving up a part of its soul. Only beneath its streets do the dark places linger; here are remnants from past centuries that haven't been renovated or modernized, structures that have been left to age alone in the dark.

My first forays into the New York underground were not to document tunnels, seek out the homeless, or write graffiti, but simply to venture into a world that would throw me for a loop. The subterranean environment was wild, unpredictable, not subject to the societal rules that reigned topside. It seemed incredibly desolate

*Figure 1.2  A disused control tower beneath the City Hall area*

*Figure 1.3  Obsolete freight tracks below mid-Manhattan*

and yet alive. Obviously people were passing through, but rarely would they show themselves as I wandered around.

But they left traces, including peculiar objects that remained, collecting dust, and coming across these was like entering a kind of fantasy realm, where the unexpected lay behind every turn. Walking a brightly lit but abandoned subway track beneath Brooklyn, finding a plastic toy train that someone had balanced perfectly on one of the rails left me puzzled. Not far from there I saw laundry hanging on a clothesline above a train spur, the clothes swaying like ghosts in the blue tunnel light. Who had left these things behind?

What was the story behind the carton of doll furniture, still sealed in cellophane, that had been placed like a present at the foot of an emergency exit's decrepit stairs? Why was there a room next to an abandoned tunnel containing nothing but a large hook near the ceiling, a ladder, and a rope? Clearly, there were interesting things going on down here, and in the solitude and expanse of these underground spaces, every detail was magnified; there was space and time for them to make an impression.

Some of the mysteries developed into narratives. It was striking to discover, in the late 1990s, a page by the graffiti writer Revs — a large section of a tunnel wall painted pale yellow and covered with what looked like a journal entry describing a childhood episode in Brooklyn. Out of context, this bright narrative seemed completely insane so deep underground. Only later did I find out that he had written more than 200 of these autobiographical pages all across the city's subway tunnels. Obviously there was a lot more going on here than met the eye.

There were also architectural oddities, and again, the deeper I delved, the more questions surfaced. Places such as the track areas of Grand Central Terminal, with their seemingly inexplicable stairways and crawlspaces, became just as intriguing as the derelict remnants of the city's first aqueduct. How astonishing to discover the sheer scope and intricacies of these man-made burrows.

Getting to the bottom of these mysteries, however, has become virtually impossible in recent years, as the shadow of the terror attacks on 9/11 has spread into all manner of subterranean spaces. The creative anarchy of earlier times has largely dissipated as security has tightened. The attacks have had a profound effect on New York's underworld, an area that now seems rife with threats. Here, in an uninhabited realm, dark and unfamiliar to most New Yorkers, the city appears particularly vulnerable.

In response, the underground is being policed like never before. Hatches have been sealed, subaquatic tunnels are guarded, and cameras have been installed. Information is disappearing off Web sites, archives are closing to the public, and photographers of infrastructure are increasingly met with suspicion. I was lucky to have discovered nearly all of the spaces in this book before the terror attacks and to have found a few kindred

*Figure 1.4  A subway tunnel beneath Chinatown*

*Figure 1.5  The abandoned water pipe inside the High Bridge*

spirits among those who work below the streets, since it is now a bad idea to venture into the city's tunnels. Yet, my desire to transform a few of these areas into playgrounds for the imagination has not left.

A friend and I first began organizing scavenger hunts and other games in underground and ruined locations under the name Dark Passage in 1999. Three years later, I founded the preservation society Ars Subterranea, with the goal of introducing the public to more unusual underground spaces. And when we curated an art exhibition on subterranean New York inside the Atlantic Avenue Tunnel in 2002, the overwhelming amount of visitors demonstrated the public interest in this subject. Many spaces that would have been accessible to us only a few years ago are now closed to cultural events, but we will continue trying.

This book is rooted in the same motives — a passion for tunnels and a love for New York's underground. While it is intended as a fairly comprehensive overview of what lies below our streets, my attention has leaned toward the stories of people who have creatively broken new ground, such as the inventor Alfred Ely Beach, the sandhog Dick Creedon, the caver Chris Beauchamp, and the writer Revs. It is meant as an armchair guide to the city's nether worlds, not as an invitation for exploration, and that is why no private entry locations will be revealed.

The abundance of myths and legends that have sprung up about New York's underground is not surprising — about sewer inspectors who arm themselves with rifles and go on subterranean alligator hunts; about a forgotten subway station with chandeliers and fountains, where an old woman plays piano at night; about cathedral-like spaces hewn out of the granite far below ground. Most of these myths have their origins in historic events covered in this book.

As this world becomes increasingly shut to New York's public, I expect the legends will only grow in scope and embellishment. In the underground, at least, New York will always retain its mysteries.

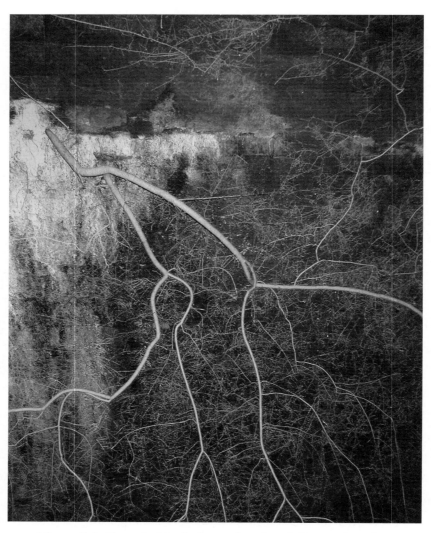

*Figure 2.1  Roots inside the long-abandoned Croton Aqueduct in the Bronx*

CHAPTER TWO
# A City Built on Treacherous Rock

"New York is a city that eats its history," Gerard Koeppel, author of *Water for Gotham*, wrote in 2002. As the finance capital of the world, the city has a long-standing reputation for being driven primarily by its quest for profits. Archaeologists and historians whose research depends on access to specific sites have traditionally had a difficult time in New York. Until the terror attacks on the World Trade Center slowed down developments in lower Manhattan, property values, not historic merit, set the standard for the use of many particular locations. Any archaeological excavation in downtown Manhattan, which could stifle the cash flow or obstruct rent collection, would have to fall by the wayside. Each hole in the ground needed to be covered as quickly as possible, each construction site transformed into rentable property.

In their book *Unearthing Gotham*, the archaeologists Anne-Marie Cantwell and Diana diZerega Wall address the reluctance of New Yorkers to integrate New York's historical background into the collective identity of the city. To many of its residents, New York is the emblem of progress; digging in the past is something best left to other, more sluggish towns. That the city's history is nonetheless being rediscovered and preserved is a relatively new phenomenon. As recently as 1963, barely anyone turned out to protest the demolition of the original Pennsylvania Station, and only when the monumental concourse had disappeared, to be replaced by the infinitely less attractive Madison Square Garden, did New Yorkers wake up. In 1965 the New York City Landmarks Commission was created partially in response to the ensuing public furor, just in time to save Grand Central Terminal from a similar destruction. In recent decades, New York developed a greater awareness of its historic relics and is paying closer attention to discoveries that anchor the city in its past.

A large part of these discoveries are made in the underground. The city's oldest colonial artifact, a coin from the year 1590, was found by an archaeologist at a construction site in 1983. In the course of those excavations on Broad Street, the foundation wall of a tavern and a cistern from the seventeenth century also appeared, and, as part of the Stadt Huys project, are now being displayed below glass next to the finished building. The restoration of City Hall Park in the late 1990s yielded a staggering amount of artifacts and human remains just below the lawn, which have helped shed light on life in the colonial era.

Yet the recently awakened historic interest still has to compete with New York's self-image as the world's economic capital. Even as the public increasingly respects the underground as a potential treasure chest of artifacts, the rent needs to be collected, and fast. But New York's conflicted connection to its own underground goes even deeper. For centuries the city has carried on a well-documented love-hate relationship with its geological foundation, the rock bottom that allows a skyscraper's verticality in both the upward and downward directions. The solidity of the rock has permitted structural engineers to achieve record-breaking heights, yet the engineering feats that had to be accomplished just in trying to reach that rock have been no less pioneering. The geology of New York can always be counted on for a surprise: solid granite borders on decayed rock and quicksand in ways that are unpredictable and often dangerous.

The city primarily rests on a hard rock called Manhattan schist. Although its consistency is very tough, it is prone to decay, making tunnel construction especially perilous. Not all of Manhattan is well suited to support heavy buildings, and the idiosyncrasies of the rock foundation can be spotted from the surface by what might seem like a haphazard distribution of skyscrapers. Constructing a high-rise

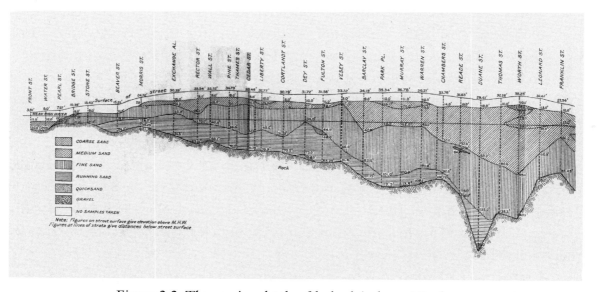

*Figure 2.2  The varying depths of bedrock in lower Manhattan*

above Houston Street in the East Village, for instance, would mean that engineers would have to dig more than 100 feet down in order to find the gneiss to support the structure. At Rockefeller Center, in contrast, the schist is so close to the street surface that it had to be blasted to make room for garages and basements.

Manhattan, an island of roughly 23 square miles, has several distinct topographic areas. The small hills that once speckled lower Manhattan were evened out in the course of city development — during the filling in of the old Collect Pond, for example. Toward upper Manhattan, the rock formations and hills become more apparent; north of Central Park the city is home to large ridges and fault lines. The highest point in Manhattan is at 185th Street, about 270 feet above sea level. Conversely — since the subway runs at a fairly level grade, even as the street altitude rises — the 191st Street station is the deepest in the New York subway system, lying 180 feet below ground.

Among the five boroughs comprising New York City, Manhattan is the one whose physical shape has changed the most in the last few centuries. Since the first settlers moved here in the sixteenth century, downtown Manhattan has grown

*Figure 2.3 These building supports on West 123rd Street rest on bedrock above street level*

by one third of its original area, mainly through deposits of soil and waste products. During the construction of the World Trade Center alone, about 1.2 million cubic yards of soil were excavated and deposited into the Hudson, creating an entire new neighborhood, Battery Park City. For foundation engineers, it can be a nightmare having to process these accumulated deposits before finding solid rock.

Subterranean construction is further complicated by underground rivers. That the city is riddled with streams buried deep beneath the pavement may conjure up images of romantic, cavernous grottoes straight out of Jules Verne. Unfortunately, these do not exist. But the waterways that have carved their beds into Manhattan's soil are still affected by tidal changes and continue to drive contractors to despair. Because they have been obstructed by building foundations does not mean they have lost their vitality.

These waterways used to run largely above ground before gradually being forced beneath the surface during the urban development of Manhattan. The water of what the early settlers called Turtle Creek, for example, contributes to a lake in Central Park, dips below 59th Street and the Metro-North train tracks under Park

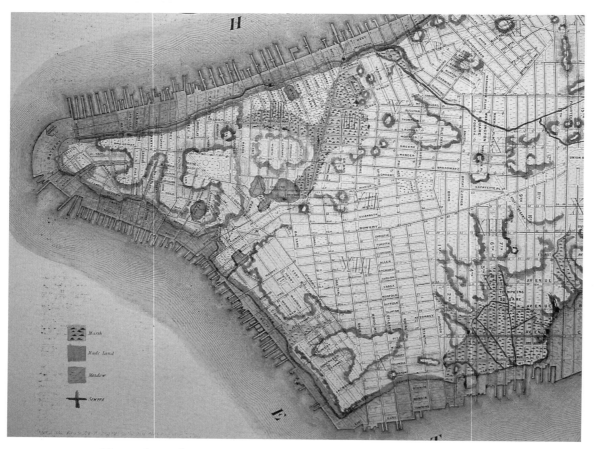

*Figure 2.4  The Viele map traces subterranean streams in New York*

Avenue, until emerging in the East River in an area once called Turtle Bay, presently the site of the United Nations. Maiden Lane in lower Manhattan was named after the young women washing their laundry in the brook running along that street, while Cedar Creek flowed from a duck pond at Madison Square through Gramercy Park to the East River. The Stuyvesant Meadows and their various streams occupied a marshland area from Avenue A to the East River between Houston and 12th streets, where the water table still needs to be kept in check during any new construction. In Harlem, there were so many small streams that in the seventeenth and eighteenth centuries it was possible to travel from the Hudson to the East River by canoe.

Until the early nineteenth century, Minetta Brook flowed into the Hudson near Greenwich Village. The residents lucky enough to live beside this idyllic creek were able to catch the best trout in all of Manhattan here. Less pleasant was a large area of marshland surrounding the brook, which had been turned into a mass grave for slaves and yellow fever victims in the 1790s. When it was transformed into Washington Square Park in the 1820s, the swamp yielded more than 10,000 human remains. To dry out the soil during the park construction, the riverbed was diverted and forced underground. Today, a small street called Minetta Lane in the heart of Greenwich Village follows the course of the stream flowing beneath the pavement. The volatile creek — once referred to as "Devil's Water" — still occasionally floods the basements along its route.

Since subterranean streams in New York continue to dictate the plans of construction engineers, a topographical atlas by Egbert L. Viele from 1865 remains one of the most essential reference tools. Viele, a civil engineer, began tracing the city's watercourses in 1860, as many of the creek beds were already disappearing beneath buildings, often with dire results. "It is seriously to be regretted that the engineers who laid out this city did not know that the streams then observable on the island were fed by perennial springs," he mentioned to a newspaper in 1892. "They made the fatal mistake of not providing a system of drains to carry off this living water that is constantly bubbling out of the rocks on which the city is built, and which will find an outlet somehow."

Viele's concern was that the streams for which no proper drainage had been provided were spreading diseases, and as the sanitary engineer of Central Park, he helped design an elaborate drainage system 18 miles long, which prevented the buildup of contaminated groundwater. But his astonishingly precise topographical map is valued by structural engineers to this day for the simple reason that it prevents their excavations from ending in disaster. When the chief engineer for the Chase Manhattan Plaza decided to forego Viele's map during the plaza's construction in 1957, his crew was unprepared for the fact that the building site lay directly over a stream, which had caused an accumulation of quicksand. To salvage the site and keep the water out of the foundations, a barrier of silicic gel had to be injected into the mud for the first time in the construction history of New York.

Not only live streams but even entire ships have been found in New York's underground. During the excavations for the Cortlandt Street subway station in 1916, the workers suddenly came across the remains of an old vessel. James Kelly, their foreman, happened to be a history buff, and he was excited by the find. Nearby Greenwich Street had originally been right on the Hudson's shore, and Kelly was convinced that the ship lying before him in the underground belonged to a group of vessels that had arrived here from the Netherlands in 1613. One of their number, a ship called Tijger, had burned down just off the coast of West Manhattan. Although the archaeologists he contacted did not seem to share his enthusiasm, he had the prow sawed off and removed to a large aquarium. A subsequent analysis of the wood, now displayed by the Museum of the City of New York, revealed that it did in fact stem from the years between 1450 and 1610.

But only the part of the ship obstructing the subway dig was salvaged. The remainder, along with all the other old artifacts (a cannon ball, tools, pipes, shards) were reburied. Although archaeologists were assigned to look for the vessel when the area was excavated again during the construction of the World Trade Center, they were unable to locate the rest of the ship.

Today it is not as easy to rebury artifacts of historic value. Since the introduction of the National Historic Preservation Act in 1966, every construction site in New York that is at least partially funded by the government has to be examined by an archaeologist, and each unearthed artifact needs to be documented. Of course it is still possible for construction companies to hire archaeologists whose loyalty doesn't necessarily lie on the side of historic discovery and who might try to obscure any finds that could potentially shut down the building site and incur momentous financial losses.

The regulation of 1966 does, however, give the city a unique opportunity to find out more about its past. One significant find was made in 1991 at a construction site on the corner of Duane Street and Broadway, at what has since been known as the African Burial Ground, where the General Services Administration was planning to build an office tower. Archaeologists unearthed hundreds of human remains from the eighteenth century at this forgotten cemetery, which is believed to have contained up to 20,000 bodies beneath a 20-foot layer of landfill. The skeletons, many of which turned out to be those of slaves, were numbered and photographed

*Figure 2.5  Rebuilding the foundation of 7 World Trade Center in 2003*

before temporarily being transferred into boxes, until, over a year later, the property owners put an end to an exhumation that had cost more than 20 million dollars.

As a result of the preservation efforts of several African American groups, the GSA set aside an area for the reburial of the human remains, which, in the meantime, were stored in the basement of 6 World Trade Center, with artifacts and documentation, until they were beset by an unexpected turn of events. Fortunately, despite the structural devastation in the area, this project did not become another casualty of the terrorist attacks on 9/11. New crypts were constructed to receive the coffins, and in October 2003, the remains were finally returned to their resting place.

part I Utilities

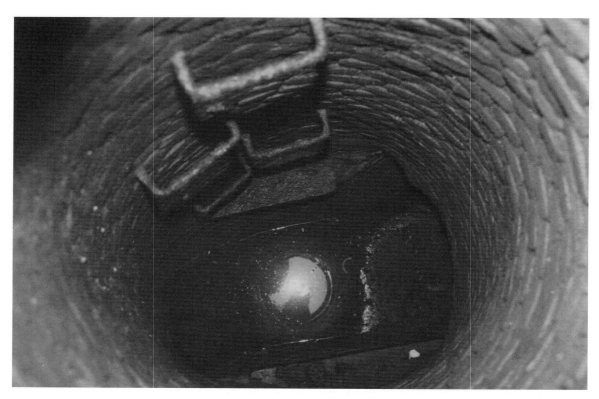

*Figure 3.1  A manhole leading to a branch of the former Croton Aqueduct in Soho*

# CHAPTER THREE

# Struggling for Fresh Water

There is a small street in Soho that is barely longer than an alley and, surprisingly, contains no stores. Few people would probably guess that a manhole in the pavement of Jersey Street drops straight into one of the relics of New York City's first aqueduct. The brick-lined conduit below a manhole cover from 1866 is part of a network that stretches from Lower Manhattan all the way to the Croton River in the north.

New York has never had it easy in its procurement of fresh water. The Hudson River, which branches into the East River south of the Bronx, consists of salt water in the city's vicinity, leaving Manhattan with few options. The early settlers built the first public well in 1677 near the fort at Bowling Green, and for the next hundred years, much of the drinking water was distributed by pumps placed at various street corners. The largest direct water supply was the Collect Pond, which once took up a considerable area around what is now Foley Square.

The Collect Pond was the size of several city blocks and so deep that up until the eighteenth century it was believed to contain sea monsters — and patriotic ones at that — as they were said to have captured at least one British soldier trying to swim across during the Revolution. The lake, which even had a small island in its center, was originally surrounded by rolling hills and tranquil meadows. But like Manhattan's creeks, it became hopelessly contaminated, and as sanitary conditions deteriorated toward the end of the eighteenth century, drinking from the Collect Pond became a health risk. Yet the city's residents, desperately thirsty, had no other recourse. A yellow fever epidemic in 1798, spread by foul water, took so many lives among the then 60,000 New Yorkers that the public increasingly began to clamor for a remedy.

Among the many proposals for new water systems received by the city, that of Aaron Burr was among the most highly regarded. It was a somewhat primitive undertaking: the pipes were to be fashioned from hollow tree trunks, running

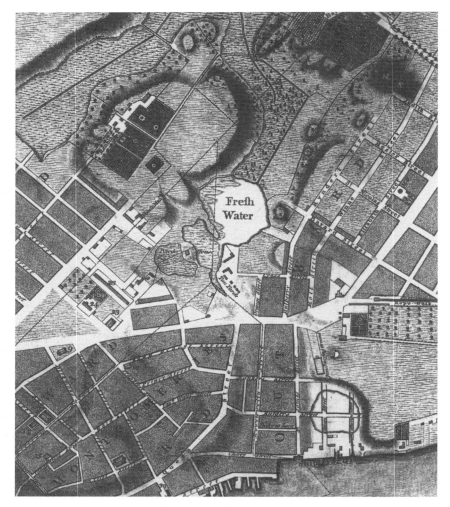

*Figure 3.2    Until it was drained in 1803, the Collect (Fresh Water) Pond supplied increasingly contaminated drinking water*

from a reservoir on Chambers Street directly to those houses in lower Manhattan that were willing to pay for the service. In 1799, Burr's Manhattan Company received city funds to install its pipes below the streets. But providing a new water supply was only of secondary interest to Burr, who sought to profit from the venture. He ignored his pledge to bring in fresh water from an untapped source north of lower Manhattan and instead built new pumps to divert the contaminated water from the Collect Pond to the reservoir on Chambers Street. In the end, although some households did connect to his water system, Burr used the remaining funds to start a financial institution, today's Chase Manhattan Bank.

New Yorkers continued to resort to wells; one shaft that was dug at Broadway and Bleecker Street in 1832 descended more than 400 feet before reaching an underground stream. Not far from there, at Broadway and 13th Street, the groundwater was tapped specifically for the fire companies, who had a hard time trying to quell the frequent blazes. But in 1835, a devastating fire ripped through the city and destroyed around 700 buildings, including historic houses of the first Dutch settlers. This at last brought some urgency to the search for water, and the city decided to tap the Croton River north of Manhattan by building a long water tunnel that would feed two large new reservoirs.

In 1837, work was begun on the forty-one-mile-long Croton Aqueduct. From the north, the masonry tunnel wound past Ossining through a forest in the Bronx, passing into Manhattan across the High Bridge and then descending toward the Receiving Reservoir in what would become Central Park, and the Distributing Reservoir on Fifth Avenue and 42nd Street. From this reservoir on Murray Hill a network of pipes ran like arteries through the city. The tunnel, which was built on a downward grade across its entire course, is still considered one of the great engineering marvels of the modern world.

The inauguration of this enormous system in 1842 included an unusual journey: a small skiff with four passengers, the "Croton Maid," accompanied the first flow of water through the tunnel. It took two days for the water to make its way to City Hall, where its arrival was greeted with much cheer and excitement in the greatest public celebration the city had ever experienced.

Yet this new resource could not quench New York's thirst for long. Between 1860 and 1912, more than 25 million immigrants passed through the city, and what had seemed like an extravagant water supply soon felt like a mere trickle. Additional

*Figure 3.3 Construction of the South Gate House in Central Park*

*Figure 3.4 The old Croton Aqueduct was supplemented by a new water tunnel in 1885*

reservoirs were created along the Croton River, while the Receiving Reservoir was enlarged and restructured to appear like a natural lake inside the new Central Park. Finally the excavations for the New Croton Aqueduct, running parallel to the original line, were started in 1885.

Soon afterward, the city designated another fresh water source in the Catskill Mountains, although a formidable obstacle — the Hudson River — separated this otherwise ideal supply from the city. The high volume of ship traffic made the construction of another bridge impractical. Instead, a tunnel was built beneath the Hudson, achieving another engineering milestone. Below the river, the aqueduct had to be carved through solid granite at a depth of nearly 1,200 feet — almost as deep as the Empire State Building is tall.

While one construction crew worked its way south from the Catskills, another was moving north from Manhattan, preparing the underground pipes. In January 1914, a final blast 450 feet below 150th Street joined both sides of the water system. Now, at least in theory, it was possible to walk the entire length of the tunnel from the Catskills to Brooklyn, a journey that was actually attempted.

To the great amusement of the sandhogs who had worked on the tunnel, a group of seven journalists and two photographers set out on a hundred-mile hike through the aqueduct on January 19, 1914, accompanied by one of the tunnel engineers. Although they were warned about alpine drops of more than 1,000 feet, the group

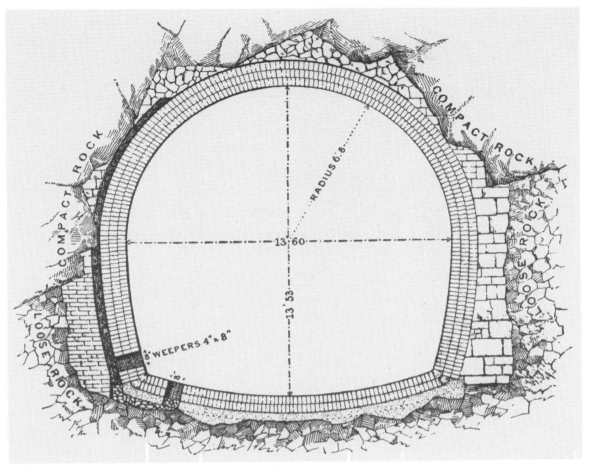

*Figure 3.5  The horseshoe-shape construction of much of the city's first two water tunnels facilitated
the flow of nonpressurized water*

entered the tunnel near Kingston, expecting to cover 13 miles on their first day. They did
not make it very far. After encountering a 500-foot siphon filled with water, they gave
up within a few miles of their starting point.

City Water Tunnel No. 1, which was built as the local section of this massive
aqueduct, was first put into use in 1917 and together with the New Croton Aqueduct
and City Water Tunnel No. 2, which was finished in 1936, it still supplies New
York's water to this day. The original Croton Aqueduct was finally closed in 1955.
The Murray Hill Reservoir made way for the New York Public Library, and the
Receiving Reservoir was filled in to become the Great Lawn.

Today the city's two main water tunnels are fed by three aqueducts further north —
the New Croton, Catskill, and Delaware — and carry a much higher volume of
water into the city than they did at their inception. Most parts of the system are
aging; only recently an unmanned submarine was sent through a 45-mile segment

*Figure 3.6  A gate chamber in the New Croton Aqueduct*

of the leaking Delaware Aqueduct, recording the state of its deterioration as part of a long-term maintenance project. If one of these main arteries were to fail, the results could be devastating. As New Yorkers well know, the smaller water mains that crisscross the city have been prone to occasional bursts for some time. Much damage was caused by a blown conduit in Washington Heights in October 2003, and during another dramatic burst on Fifth Avenue in January 1998, an entire car was swallowed by a hole in the street.

The large main beneath Fifth Avenue is particularly prone to a blowout. But the brittle, four-foot-wide tube that was first installed in the 1870s can't be taken out of commission without causing a water shortage. The Department of Environmental Protection is planning to reactivate an obsolete main beneath Madison Avenue for the repair work on Fifth Avenue, which itself requires maintenance. Like a cranky old hospital patient, the city's water system is continually demanding attention.

Figure 3.7  Men at work inside the New Croton Aqueduct

Figure 3.8  City Water Tunnel No. 2 was constructed with a diameter of 19 feet

*Figure 3.9  Sealed water pipes in the abandoned Ridgewood Reservoir, Brooklyn*

Since the 1960s, New York has had a mammoth backup plan in the form of a third water tunnel. This 60-mile-long aqueduct will supplement the water supply in Queens and Brooklyn and enable the temporary closure of the other water tunnels for overdue repair work. In 1970 the construction was started, and aside from a temporary hiatus later that decade, the excavations have been proceeding ever since.

The work on City Water Tunnel No. 3 is in progress at several city locations at once, such as at one prominent construction site on 30th Street and 10th Avenue in Manhattan, where a small elevator cage descends into a shaft 600 feet deep. In its broadest sections, the tunnel is carved out of the rock by the "Mole," an awe-inspiring piece of machinery equipped with a huge cutting wheel that creates a circular passage. The excavations have taken their toll on the sandhogs, who have described the tunnel as a man-a-mile job, which means, on average, that one life is lost per completed mile. So far, 24 workers have died in the 24 miles of tunnel.

One larger segment of the tunnel was already put into use in 1998, connecting the Hillview Reservoir to Queens by way of Central Park, and permitting the closure of sections of the other two water tunnels. The opening of that stretch concludes the first of the four planned construction stages. The entire project is not expected to be finished until 2030. In the meantime, the excavation pits will continue to appear at street corners, their inconspicuous exteriors giving no indication of the incredible work taking place hundreds of feet beneath.

*Figure 4.1  The spine of the old Croton Aqueduct emerges along a trail in the Bronx*

CHAPTER FOUR

# In the Wake of the Croton Maid

The remnants of the old Croton Aqueduct still lie beneath the city, its winding masonry tube rotting away in desolation. It is New York's most magnificent ruin. When it was still accessible, it was possible to walk on foot from the Bronx into Manhattan. Yet the narrow entrance that allowed such a journey, discovered by cavers long ago, has since been barricaded by a landslide of leaves and branches. This once vital artery, burrowing through the skin of the city, has been claimed by nature as its own.

Where the tunnel enters the city from the north, its masonry spine occasionally pokes through the ground, as the Aqueduct Trail leads on top of the tunnel's roof through an overgrown forest in Van Cortlandt Park, passing a waste weir along the way. The aqueduct's chief engineer, John B. Jervis, had designed the waterworks in the 1830s along the lines of ancient Egyptian architecture, since he was impressed with its simple forms and hoped that his masterpiece was equally destined for eternity. The weir, which reflects this simplicity, houses a large iron gate that was once used to regulate the water flow, making it possible to shut off this section of the tunnel. It is the only one of the six original weir chambers that can still be found in the city; likewise, most of the vent stacks, which once protruded like small turrets from the ground, have disappeared.

Most of the tunnel section leading from the Bronx to the High Bridge contains an uncomfortable amount of stagnant water, which at one point reaches a depth of three feet. The constant prospect of slipping on a layer of gray mud makes walking through this tube all the more interesting. An underground hike through the Bronx is by no means monotonous. Bats and stalactites line the ceiling, and the masonry is perforated by roots resembling anatomical diagrams. Underneath the Jerome Reservoir, where the new and old aqueduct meet, are narrow chambers with rusted pumps. Whenever the tunnel passes below a street, the sound of cars driving across the metal manhole covers echoes ominously through the passage.

*Figure 4.2  The old and new Croton Aqueducts meet at the Jerome Park Reservoir*

*Figure 4.3  A wall with a small opening blocks the water tunnel as it enters the High Bridge
in the Bronx*

Close to the High Bridge, the tunnel abruptly plunges into the ground and it suddenly becomes clear why the aqueduct was a favorite spot for cavers. Traversing this passage and ascending on the other side is next to impossible without a rope, unless one wants to slide into a pile of debris that has accumulated at its bottom throughout the past decades. Once the descent is navigated, another challenge awaits. The tunnel's connection to the High Bridge consists of a very tight opening barely high enough to crawl through.

Seen from the inside out, the High Bridge, which was finished in 1848, is one of the most beautiful structures in the city. Jervis, who initially favored a lower, more economical crossing, decided on a bridge design based on the old Roman aqueducts that would not impede ship traffic. It was to serve not only as a water conduit but as a pedestrian crossing. This, New York City's very first bridge, was to become an important public link between Manhattan and the Bronx.

The construction of the bridge, which lasted from 1838 to 1848, was a challenge. The riverbed was unstable, filled with loose boulders and the remains of an old ship, and Jervis was forced to set the piers on wooden pylons sunk into the ground. But New Yorkers were enchanted. Even before its completion, the High Bridge had

*Figure 4.4  The gate chamber on the Bronx side of the High Bridge*

become a popular tourist destination. On Sundays, people donned their finery and walked along the riverbanks, admiring the structure rising from the waters in the idyllic, overgrown landscape. Edgar Allan Poe, then a Bronx resident, wrote about his walks along the site of the bridge and it became the subject of numerous paintings, the most famous of which was finished by Currier and Ives in 1849. As anticipated, the new pedestrian crossing was linking neighborhoods and fueling new construction on both sides of the river.

In the early twentieth century, the High Bridge was threatened with demolition, because the stone piers were obstructing the increasing ship traffic along the Harlem River. Instead, five of the original piers were removed and replaced by a broad steel arch. Since the aqueduct became obsolete and the pedestrian walkway was closed for security reasons (four passengers on a ship were injured by stones tossed from the span in 1958) the bridge has been slumbering behind locked gates.

Its neglected state is what makes the interior of the High Bridge all the more spectacular. On each side of the overpass, both in the Bronx and Manhattan, a gate chamber has been buried in the hillside, through which the water conduit makes its transition between the underground and the bridge. These transition areas are particularly intriguing, since there are several rooms and tunnel stubs whose original purposes are difficult to reconstruct, especially because they have been altered over the years. Stairs lead to sealed doors, small chambers contain blocked drains and rusted valves, and there is one large siphon that plunges deep into the ground. This siphon, which is buried in the Bronx hillside, turned out to be quite dangerous the first time we entered this space.

*Figure 4.5 A postcard of the High Bridge before its western piers were replaced by a steel arch*

My friends and I discovered it accidentally: a smooth masonry tube barely six feet in diameter, which snaked away from the bridge before making a steep descent. Chris found it first. While we were climbing around the two-leveled structure of the gate chamber, he followed what seemed to be just a short tunnel branching off to the side. But as he turned the corner, we suddenly heard a shout and a low rumbling noise as he rapidly slid several hundred feet into a dark hole. We arrived to watch his headlamp trace his downward path, becoming more faint by the second.

Then, Chris, an experienced caver who lives precisely for these situations, slowly came crawling back up. He reported that his journey ended in a pitch-black space, barely four feet high, which was filled with dark mud and mysterious metal objects that seemed obviously intent on spearing him. From there the tunnel narrowed further and apparently sumped out. Needless to say, his slide into the pit had to be extensively recreated by the rest of us over several return trips, until I finally took it too fast and ended up in the emergency room. But that's another story.

Chris took advantage of another promising feature of the High Bridge, namely, its hollow piers. Because the stone piers had to rest on the wooden pylons in the river, Jervis decided to make them as light as possible. Their interiors are open, with

*Figure 4.6  A masonry siphon plunges from the gate chamber into the Bronx hillside*

*Figure 4.7 With an increasing demand for water, the two original pipes were replaced by a much larger iron tube*

the thick walls only supported by horizontal stone braces. They have small holes at the bottom designed to drain any overflow into the river. Some of these shafts can be accessed from the walkway inside the bridge, and it was not long until Chris and our friend Gary began rappelling into the piers.

Originally the water was carried across the bridge in two masonry tubes, each three feet in diameter, but because the city's water requirements quickly surpassed all expectations, a seven-foot-wide iron pipe was installed in 1860. This metal tube is now filled with flakes of rust; it is so perforated that when walking on the inside, the sunlight enters the dark space through a constellation of small holes resembling a starlit sky. The first time we walked along here we found an animal skeleton, presumably of a small dog, which had fallen apart completely undisturbed — evidence of how destitute the interior of this bridge has been.

On the Bronx side, the metal pipe is enclosed in the original stone housing of the bridge, which leaves ample room for a walkway alongside it. Where the piers have been replaced with the steel arch, the tube is supported by a metal lattice with catwalks on each side. At the Manhattan end of the catwalks is another chamber containing the two original pipes that used to lead up into the water tower, which still stands on a cliff above the bridge.

The High Bridge tower was built in 1872 to stabilize the pressure inside the tunnel and provide water to upper Manhattan, which lies too far above the aqueduct's grade to be supplied directly from the tunnel. At the top of the tower was a water tank with a capacity of 47,000 gallons; when this did not suffice, a reservoir was completed next door a year later and has since been turned into a swimming pool. Unfortunately the tower has been locked off from the public following a fire set by a homeless person in 1984. The ornate iron staircase winding around the two interior water conduits makes for a very striking space.

From about 173rd to 135th streets in northern Manhattan, the aqueduct is still intact below the streets. Because no one was allowed to build on top of the tunnel, its course can be followed on the street surface with the help of indicators such as water hydrants, manhole covers, and pumps. The longest straight section runs below Amsterdam Avenue, along which were built a number of gate houses, all but

*Figure 4.8  The High Bridge Water Tower overlooks the Harlem River*

three of which have been demolished. The houses at 135th Street and 119th Street are inconspicuous classic structures in somewhat ruinous states; both are awaiting new futures as cultural centers.

Just before curving toward the gatehouse on 135th Street, the unobstructed tunnel path ends, and its traces on the surface likewise lose themselves. From the reservoir in Central Park, the main line runs below Fifth Avenue, and occasional manhole covers still mark its path. After the reservoir at Murray Hill was torn down to make room for the public library, the aqueduct's other remnants were swallowed by the city.

The long subterranean passage between the High Bridge and 135th Street resembles that in the Bronx, but is all the more exciting just by virtue of being below Manhattan. The sense of unreality intensifies in this section of the tunnel. It is very moist, pockets of fog obscure the opening ahead, and each sound seems to travel for a mile before echoing back. Beyond the gate chamber, where the masonry tunnel resumes its downtown course, there is a flooded shaft, which lies beneath a sealed manhole to the Highbridge Park. On a ledge behind this shaft sits an incongruous object, two porcelain hands folded in prayer. Perhaps someone died here, and this sets an eerie tone for the journey ahead.

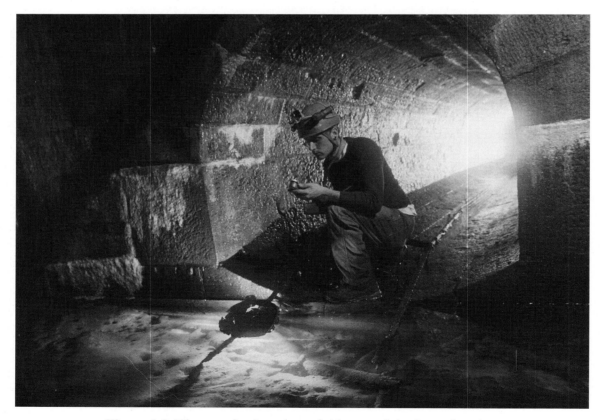

*Figure 4.9  The aqueduct's nooks and side tunnels invite exploration*

*Figure 4.10 Constructed in the 1890s, the gatehouse on 119th Street is now obsolete*

*Figure 4.11 An adventurous inspection of the New Croton Aqueduct*

After walking for a while, any sense of time disappears. As in the Bronx section, roots are clinging to the masonry amidst the stalactites, and a subway train rumbles by seemingly next door. There is a good opportunity to view a tunnel section blasted out of the Manhattan schist; dynamite tracks perforate the walls all the way to the ceiling, which in this segment has been left entirely as natural rock. During a period in 1910, when the aqueduct was closed, two workers etched graffiti into the tunnel floor. The grade of the tunnel is more noticeable in Manhattan, and by the time the end is reached at 135th Street, the water is waist high. At the end of the tunnel a series of rusted ladders leads to the street. Glancing up through the openings in the manhole cover for the first time, with cars speeding by directly over my head, I felt like a creature from another world.

Jervis's aqueduct ruins, with all their mysterious shafts, siphons, pumps, and chambers, are my favorite spot in New York, and to pay homage to its illustrious history, my friends Chris Beauchamp and Aaron Benoy and I decided to re-create at least a part of the voyage of the Croton Maid. The Croton Maid was the small skiff that accompanied the flow of the first water through the aqueduct in 1842, carrying four people. Back then the journey took two days; we decided to take one night.

On a particularly cold night some years ago, we carried an inflatable boat all the way down the tunnel toward about 155th Street, where the water was at least a foot deep. With a fair amount of beer, we christened the boat "The Croton Maid Jr." Two

*Figure 4.12 A leisurely swim far below the streets of Manhattan*

people could sit inside without sinking into the muddy water, and Aaron waded ahead, while Chris and I slowly followed in the boat.

Aside from our voices and the trickling of water, it was completely quiet. We passed beneath thick dangling roots and through heavy patches of fog. After a few hours, thoroughly frozen but in good spirits, we reached the end of the line below 135th Street. Now we could imagine what it must have been like for those four men on their maiden voyage in 1842, paving the way for future boating in Manhattan's underground.

Here's to you, John Jervis, for continuing to enrich the lives of a few New Yorkers for so many years.

*Figure 4.13  The Croton Maid Jr. awaits her passengers*

*Figure 5.1  The construction of the city's subway necessitated the replacement of many sewer lines*

# CHAPTER FIVE

# An Alligator Marks the Sewers

In early February 1935 it was snowing heavily in New York, and on 123rd Street near the Harlem River several men were busy with their shovels. One of them, Salvatore Condulucci, saw an open sewer manhole and decided it was an ideal place to dump the snow. After a while he peeked into the opening to see if it was filling up and noticed that something was moving down there. Condulucci yelled for his friends to come over, and when he saw a large form break through the snow, he jumped back and shouted, "Honest, it's an alligator!"

Incredulously, the others joined him and saw that there really was a large animal down the manhole, struggling to free itself from piles of snow. They decided to help. In the nearby Lehigh Stove and Repair Shop they bought a clothesline, made a slipknot, and managed to heave the creature ten feet to the surface. Then they admired their discovery. It was an authentic alligator — and a large one at that. Unfortunately the reptile was not used to the cold New York climate. Starved, almost frozen, it opened its mouth and snapped its jaws. The sight of the sharp teeth scared its rescuers; they took their shovels and beat the animal until it was dead.

Then they hauled the alligator into the Lehigh Stove and Repair Shop, where it was promptly weighed — 125 pounds. It was almost eight feet long. At once the store was filled with curious neighbors who tried to determine where the animal could have come from, until it was decided that it had fallen off a steamer from Florida and crawled into one of the sewer conduits toward the city. Everyone seemed satisfied with this explanation, and the crowd dispersed. Later a sanitation truck came and unceremoniously took the carcass to a dump.

This was how it was reported by the *New York Times* the next morning — and it is still the most famous story about the city's sewers. Since then the urban legend of alligators roaming beneath New York City's streets has flourished, occasionally beefed up by unverified reports of further sightings. It was not until more than half a century later, in the summer of 2001, that another alligator made an unexpected public appearance

*Figure 5.2 No New York household is complete without a sewergator*

in the waters of Manhattan, yet the myth has persisted in various manifestations: in novels, such as Thomas Pynchon's *V*, movies, comics, and other pop culture media. The novelty store Archie McPhee's sells a pale "New York Sewergator" and the Web site sewergator.com has compiled an entertaining variety of material on the subject.

Even the agency responsible for the city's sewer system, the Department of Environmental Protection (DEP), treats the urban legend with a sense of humor. An alligator with sunglasses is the department's mascot, and employees' special achievements are rewarded with gator pins. After all, the department's former superintendent Teddy May, nicknamed "King of the Sewers," was famous for his tales of encountering the reptiles while going for his habitual swims in the city's subterranean pipelines. He even claimed to have taken his men on entire alligator safaris.

When Charles Sturcken, then the DEP's chief of staff, was informed that a small alligator had been spotted in Central Park's Harlem Meer in 2001, he wanted to get hold of it, but not to bring it to an animal facility. "He ought to be given a home in the New York City sewers," Sturcken said. "That alligator would never survive the winter in the Harlem Meer. . . . The sewer system is much warmer and is the city's answer to a natural swamp, with 6,000 miles of tunnels and a billion gallons of water, replenished every day."

It is understandable that Sturcken sounded proud of the state of the city's sewers, because New York has come a long way in managing its waste, something it had a notoriously tough time with until the last century. It took this otherwise progressive city very long to implement reasonable hygienic standards. Only 150 years ago, New York had the dubious reputation of being America's worst-smelling city.

From the time of the earliest settlers onward, New Yorkers paid little attention to proper waste disposal, initially digging trenches in the streets to deposit their refuse in. The first larger sewer was created in the mid-seventeenth century from a creek that once flowed along what is now Broad Street. The creek bed was reinforced with wooden planks so the stream could more easily carry the mixture of waste and rainwater into the East River. This "Heere Gracht" was reminiscent of the canals in Dutch towns, but did not function well here. Rainwater, an essential part of the flushing process, was soon the smallest ingredient in the brew. On humid days the offensive vapors hung cloudlike above the creek, until it became unbearable to nearby residents, and it was reinforced with bricks and covered over.

This first enclosed sewer was only an emergency solution. All across the city, the waste kept flooding over and collecting in puddles on the streets, and pedestrians made a point to steer clear of certain areas during hot summer days. Even the six-foot-deep trenches in the middle of the roads were inadequate. Designed primarily as storm drains, they were soon clogged.

Human waste usually went into outhouses, which in wealthier neighborhoods were emptied every night by "tub men," primarily black slaves who transported the buckets to the rivers. In poorer neighborhoods, the outhouses were in terrible condition, with waste seeping into the ground even directly next to residences. By the late eighteenth century the tenements, particularly those on the Lower East Side, were filled to the bursting point with immigrant families, many of which lived in the cellars. There are stories of women hanging up laundry over their sleeping children in windowless basement rooms while the waste from the outhouses was running down the walls.

It was not surprising, then, that diseases were rampant in New York. When the city decided to fill in the contaminated Collect Pond in 1803, the subterranean stream that had previously fed the pond was directed into the larger creek that gave today's Canal Street its name. Along this path a large drain was excavated that emptied directly into the Hudson River. After the Collect Pond was filled in by leveling nearby Bunker Hill, the new ground was soon covered with houses; yet the cellars of these buildings constantly flooded, since the water could not drain fast enough along Canal Street. That a terrible smell kept lingering in the area was one of the factors in deciding to erect the Halls of Justice — the Tombs — directly on top of the former pond. In 1819, the

*Figure 5.3  Canal Street and Broadway in the early nineteenth century*

malodorous Canal Street sewer was covered over, the same year the Common Council banned the use of common sewers for the contents of privies.

A report from the Lyceum of Natural History from 1831 very matter-of-factly estimated that 100 tons of excrement were deposited into Manhattan's soil every 24 hours. The resulting contamination of the groundwater posed a great risk to public health. By then New Yorkers were so used to the foul taste of their drinking water that fresh water was greeted with suspicion. "This water is like wind — there is nothing substantial in it; nothing to bite upon," was one memorable comment.

But there was no easy remedy. The construction of sewers only made sense if there was ample water to flush them with. Yet for some time after the Croton Aqueduct first supplied such water in 1842, the problem intensified, since those who could afford to started building their own water closets, which only kept flooding.

In 1845 the Common Council reversed its earlier stance, now allowing the disposal of human and animal waste in the sewers, and permitting owners of water closets to furnish private drains to hook up to the larger conduits, although these could only accommodate liquid waste. Now the overflow reached disastrous levels. At this point 20,000 New Yorkers resided in cellar rooms, and in an attempt to halt the prevailing horrendous health conditions, the city granted itself the right to inspect any subterranean residences, passages, and vaults so that anything violating the previously unenforced sanitary code could be removed.

Even after the first subterranean pipes were constructed, they generally terminated in the underground streams rather than the collective sewers. On the waterfront, in the meantime, the refuse was mounting in offensive piles between the piers, compromising maritime traffic. Alfred Craven, one of the engineers of the Croton Aqueduct, who was promoting the construction of an organized sewer network, was sent to Europe to study regional sewer systems in an effort to expedite an efficient drainage system in New York.

There was an unwanted side effect to enclosing the sewers, namely explosions. Closing up the conduits meant that ventilation shafts had to be installed, or the air would be trapped inside, leading to occasional blasts. In 1846, the Fleet River in London, which had been diverted underground and was used as a sewer, blew up, causing entire houses to be swept away in a massive wave of sewage. While this event may sound entertaining from a distance, New Yorkers had to be careful to avoid a similar occurrence.

By 1857 less than a third of the roughly 500 miles of paved streets in New York were equipped with sewer lines, with the wealthier areas in the north faring better than the immigrant quarters downtown. Only after another cholera epidemic swept through Europe in 1865 did the city accelerate its sewer construction, hoping to forestall a similar outbreak, and with good results. By the early 1890s, New York had 464 miles of sewer lines, more than almost any other city in the world.

In 1902, Mayor Seth Low embarked on what may have been the world's first instance of driving a car through a sewer, causing the *New York Times* to proclaim that "automobiling through sewers is the very latest thing." Two cars were lowered into a 15-foot-wide conduit beneath 64th Street in Bay Ridge, which had been atmospherically lit with candles. The mayor and his entourage climbed down a ladder at Fourth Avenue and drove through the finished stretch of a pipe that, at a length of 300 miles, was

*Figure 5.4  A repair crew installs a new sewer pipe.*

intended to be the largest sewer in the world. Unfortunately, despite the newspaper's prediction, not much has been heard since of candlelight drives through sewers.

Despite the massive infrastructural improvements, the waste continued to be dumped into the rivers. The shores of Coney Island, which had up to one million beachgoers on hot summer days, were in particularly bad shape, due to the additional waste pouring into the ocean from the factories springing up on the waterfront. It was not until 1937 that the city's first sewage treatment plant was opened in Coney Island. Now, New York has 14 such facilities. One of these, the North River Treatment plant in Harlem, was greeted with such dismay by the local community that it was designed to be as inconspicuous as possible. Resting on caissons buried in the Hudson River, it has a park and recreation area on its roof.

The sewage plants today process 1.3 billion gallons of wastewater daily. New York is one of the relatively few American cities that still has a combined sewer system, which carries off waste along with stormwater. For this reason, overflow is still a problem when there are heavy rains, or during massive electrical failures, such as the blackout of August 2003, when large amounts of sewage spilled into the East River from the plant on 13th Street and Avenue D. The DEP has initiated a program to remedy this by constructing vast underground reservoirs where any runoff can be stored temporarily until water levels return to normal.

*Figure 5.5  Inside a storm drain in Queens*

Despite the precautions, New York did have its share of sewer explosions after all, particularly during the early twentieth century. One spectacular blast in June 1926 below a pier at 129th Street, where a seven-and-a-half-foot conduit emptied into the Hudson River, sent manhole covers within a three-block radius 50 feet into the air, injuring 11 people. It even twisted the freight tracks along the Hudson. The detonation was so forceful that people in the vicinity thought they were struck by an earthquake. In another incident in March 1978, a series of explosions were set off along a two-mile sewer stretch in the Bronx, also injuring 11 people. Many of these blasts were apparently caused by vapors from illegally dumped fuel. Then again, maybe they were the result of secret alligator extermination campaigns, gone horribly wrong.

Will New York ever rid itself of its urban legend about alligators? Not likely. Seeing the cheerfulness with which the little Central Park visitor was received by the public, the idea of these reptiles roaming the sewers is not something the city's residents are eager to give up. It continues to be one of the most persistent myths embellishing the history of New York's underground.

*Figure 5.6 Garbage passing through sewers often collects on ladders and grates*

*Figure 6.1 Construction work on Rector Street reveals a maze of conduits*

# CHAPTER SIX

# A Maze of Pipes Beneath the Streets

When the Statue of Liberty was inaugurated in 1886, its torch burned so brightly that the ship captains complained about the distraction, clamoring for the power to be turned down a notch. At the time, the ability to illuminate the night sky by means of electricity was still a relatively new and exciting phenomenon. Thomas Edison had dazzled the public with his first demonstration of electric lightbulbs in 1879. Three years later, his first Manhattan customers were plugged into the network provided by his power plant on Pearl Street. By 1886, 1,500 streetlights had been installed across the city.

From the very beginning of supplying the city's power, Edison wisely planned to go underground, running his cables not across poles but below the streets. He invented an insulation method to protect the wires from subterranean moisture by enveloping them with tar. Today the underground tangle of conduits and wires is notoriously dense, but at Edison's time there were few utility pipes outside of those of the water system and five gas works. These had been in tough competition with each other over supplying the streetlights, until Edison's electric lanterns put all of them out of the running.

Western Union and other telegraph enterprises, on the other hand, had strung their wires across poles. Photographs from that time period captured dense and gloomy streetscapes beneath a heavily interlaced sky as the poles of Bell Telephone, Western Union, the East River Electrical Lighting Company, and other utilities were straining under the weight of up to 300 cables per mast. Often the electric wires snapped and fell into the street, killing horses and, on rare occasions, pedestrians. Impressed by Edison's subterranean network, the city ordered all electrical cables to be moved underground in 1884. However, most utility companies — skeptical of contemporary insulation methods — simply ignored this.

This lax attitude came to an abrupt end in 1888, when a particularly severe blizzard became a historic event. Many poles were shattered in the snowstorms, their loose wires whipping across the streets. New York was completely cut off from the

*Figure 6.2  A manhole on 10th Avenue provides access for the installation of fiber optic cables*

outside world, and there was no longer any question that the utility lines had to move underground. Mayor Hugh P. Grant took along an axe as he surveyed the damage, threatening to fell the poles himself, but was stopped by the threat of a boycott by some of the utility companies. Most of those companies complied of their own accord anyway.

The final straw for the remaining poles came in October 1889. A Western Union lineman by the name of John Feeks was electrocuted on a mast near Chambers and Centre streets downtown, as thousands of pedestrians gathered around the dangling body and watched blue sparks sputtering from his mouth. The obvious dangers posed by the masts caused a public outcry, and when the mayor again rallied for underground conduits, everyone finally complied.

The utility companies experimented with their own insulation methods until the Empire City Subway Company was founded in 1891, with the goal of handling the underground relocation of all manner of cable—telegraph, telephone, and electricity. The company thrived even after the initial rush of installations; by the 1950s they maintained 9,000 manholes across the city. Their underground corridors also left room for the alarm services of the fire and police departments. Occasionally their workers provided unexpected archaeological assistance when stumbling across objects like Aaron Burr's wooden water pipes or native Indian artifacts during their excavations. Empire City, now a subsidiary of the telephone company Verizon, still owns many subterranean conduits in New York and leases a portion of these to various cable and fiber optic businesses.

The utility lines not only had to move below the pavement, but below the rivers as well. To bring its supply into Manhattan, the East River Gas Company in Queens began constructing the city's first tunnel below the East River in 1892. Not only did the riverbed pose geological challenges, but the engineers also had to deal with a major obstacle, Roosevelt Island. Blackwell's Island, as it was called then, was home to the city's unwanted, with a pauper hospital, an insane asylum, and a penitentiary. The two sections of the tunnel, begun on each shore, were supposed to meet directly below the Incurable Hospital.

According to the chief engineer's subsequent report, there was considerable doubt at first whether the tube segments were lining up properly, since the hospital's presence prevented a good view of the shaft headings. To get a better perspective, they sunk plumb lines along the tunnel shafts, whose tops were visible on the water surface. Then the engineers climbed on the roof of a waterfront brewery in Manhattan, from where they could look across the river and estimate how closely the two sections were aligned. Surprisingly this worked so well that they could be joined within an inch. On July 11, 1894, the last rock obstacle between the two

*Figure 6.3 A metal-lined section of the East River Gas Company tunnel, built in the 1890s*

tunnel segments was blasted out with dynamite — now it was possible to walk from Manhattan to Queens underground.

When the tunnel was completed, it was hailed as a great technical achievement, and the only regret expressed by the public was that it was built for gas lines rather than transportation. The tube had been equipped with a small railway, and after donning oilskins, the inaugurating party descended down the Manhattan shaft, where they boarded the little train cars, which were then pushed by employees of the gas company. In their celebratory speech, the consulting engineer William White proclaimed that "there is no tunnel the American capitalist will not go into if he can only see daylight at the other end," and the chief engineer Charles M. Jacobs cheerfully added that enough dynamite had been used during the construction to blow up the entire city of New York.

And so the first train ride beneath the East River went down in history. This tunnel still exists; today it houses not only gas lines but steam and power conduits as well. After the first, groundbreaking gas tunnel was finished, two other major underwater pipelines were constructed — from Astoria to the Bronx, and below the Gowanus Canal. All three tunnels now belong to Consolidated Edison, which owns 4,200 miles of gas mains in New York.

*Figure 6.4 A gas pipe is installed beneath the Harlem River*

A much larger network is provided by ConEd's power lines: about 92,000 miles of underground wires traverse the New York City area. But although ConEd and particularly Keyspan's Ravenswood Power Station supply most of the city's electricity, one notable holdout of self-sufficiency can still be found in Brooklyn. The Pratt Institute has been providing its own power ever since its inception in the late nineteenth century.

The power plant at Pratt Institute, a formidable red brick building with a large smokestack, has three steam-driven generators. Since 1900 these have replaced the weaker engines originally installed by Charles Pratt in 1887, five years after Edison first opened his plant on Pearl Street. They still generate direct current, as opposed to the alternating current provided by Con Edison, and their steam still heats the buildings in the winter. The generators can be seen through a cutaway floor in the basement of the powerhouse, from where the system branches out through two main tunnels.

Tending to the system since 1958 is the brilliant Conrad Milster, Pratt's chief engineer and steam aficionado. It's thanks to his efforts that the old engines have been preserved and still retain their luster. Mr. Milster does more than oil the machines; he has also salvaged parts of derelict engines and, for decades, has archived the sounds of historic steam whistles, with the idea that the sound of

*Figure 6.5 One of the three steam-driven generators at the Pratt Institute's power plant*

each machine conveys a distinct personality. On New Year's Eve, he has made it a tradition to haul out a steam calliope on the grounds of Pratt and blast its whistles at the stroke of midnight.

Although steam may seem like the by-product of an industrial age long in the past, New York still makes ample use of it. In fact, this city has the largest underground steam network in the world, coursing through iron mains six feet below the pavement. The system delivers steam to more than 1,800 buildings that lack their own heating facilities. In the summer the steam is used for cooling purposes.

In 1882 the New York Steam Company began deliveries to its first customer, the United Bank Building on Broadway and Wall Street. Only a few months later, the utility was servicing most of the financial district. Today the system belongs to Con Edison, which operates five steam plants in Manhattan and one each in Queens and Brooklyn. Roughly 1,200 manholes lead to this system, some of which can be recognized by the white vapors drifting into the streets, imparting a film noir atmosphere to the city. These are caused not by leaks in the steam mains but by the moist air that is created when subsurface water drips onto the hot pipes and evaporates. In extreme cases, the steam gets directed upward through orange and white striped plastic tubes to prevent obscuring drivers' vision.

*Figure 6.6 Insulating a steam pipe in the late 1920s*

While the steam escaping from the pavement can make it seem like something in the underground is ready to explode, flying manhole covers today are much more likely to belong to the electrical system. One such occasion is aptly illustrated in the 1970 movie *The Out of Towners*, when Jack Lemmon steps off a manhole a moment before a subterranean explosion sends the cover blasting into the air. New Yorkers know, of course, that this is no joke, and that this is an expected occurrence in the winter. According to Con Edison, such explosions are the result of faulty cables, caused by the salt on the streets that drips into the manholes with the melting snow.

What it is like to work inside these manholes was something I learned from a friend who has been employed by a telephone company for 12 years, installing fiber optic

*Figure 6.7 Vapor rising from the streets is a common sight in New York*

cables. His daily routine involves opening two adjoining manholes and pulling a yellow rope through the connecting tunnel. One end of the rope is tied to a winch, which then pulls the telephone cable from a large spool through the underground passages. Each day he and his partner can install several miles of cables.

Occasionally he has to descend into one of the subterranean chambers that house the relay switches, where the large copper cables that are connected to the central station via fiber optics are joined. Placing these facilities into the underground saves money and space, but it is also a safety measure. Even before 9/11, the exact locations of these chambers were top secret, since a terror attack in one of these rooms could cripple communications across large parts of the city. Thus, the hatches are not only well concealed but are secured by at least three locking mechanisms.

Although the chambers are equipped with electricity and ventilation shafts, they can feel claustrophobic. "For some reason, when I am in one of these, I imagine it's how it would be in a submarine," my friend says. "Closing the hatch is kinda spooky once you are down there." Nonetheless he prefers working here to the street — he even feels safer. In case of a major emergency, this is the place he would escape to. The security system makes this location safe from intruders; it is as well protected as a bunker.

Even the remnants of a pneumatic mail system can still be found below the streets of New York. A century ago, letters were sent between post offices through underground pipelines at a speed of up to 40 miles an hour. In 1897 these systems were installed in Chicago, Boston, Philadelphia, St. Louis, and New York. The line going from Battery Park to Times Square, Grand Central Terminal, and the main office at Penn Station up into Harlem was 27 miles long. The tubes were also installed across the Brooklyn Bridge to connect to the postal service in Brooklyn. Until the system was replaced by delivery vehicles, it functioned reasonably well, the occasional crash landing of misdirected mail notwithstanding.

For every direction from the post offices there was a pair of tubes for arriving and departing mail. The iron tubes had a diameter of eight inches and propelled the letter-filled canisters by means of pneumatic pressure, overseen by someone called a rocketeer. In an internal newsletter from the 1950s, the canisters were compared to artillery shells: "'mail shot from guns' may be an apt description." To prevent the individual units from jamming somewhere underground, the conduits were occasionally greased by means of oil containers sent through the pipes. The canisters also had small wheels to better handle the curves. They were routed by means of deflectors that popped up at intersections, making sure the cargo was shot into the right post office. Not only canisters but also entire parcels were sent through the system, and one unfortunate cat was reported to have gone through and survived, albeit with some dizziness.

*Figure 6.8 Inside a telephone company's underground switching center*

The possibilities of pneumatic mail distribution seemed endless. In the year 1900 the postmaster general Charles Emory Smith optimistically proclaimed that one day all households in America would be connected with each other by these tubes. Yet the system had a big disadvantage, in that the post offices could not be relocated without tearing up the streets and redirecting all the lines. It was also expensive. Each year an average of $17,000 per mile had to be invested in maintenance. In December 1953, citing financial reasons, the post office began the process of transferring its mail delivery from pneumatic tubes to trucks.

But not all pneumatic transport has been discontinued in New York. Some buildings, such as the office tower at 11 Penn Plaza, libraries, and hospitals were equipped with internal tubes. By now the glitches have been ironed out to the point that pneumatic delivery is a desirable option even for something as fragile as medical specimen, and it is used by the Columbia Presbyterian Medical Center in Manhattan and Kings County Hospital in Brooklyn. At Home Depot, pneumatic

*Figure 6.9  The Astoria gas tunnel below the East River is holed through in 1913*

tubes deliver cash to the vaults. New York City even boasts one of the world's few pneumatic garbage disposal systems — the Avac center that operates below Roosevelt Island. Here, the trash from the housing developments is sucked into underground conduits and transported to the garbage center on the northern part of the island at speeds of up to 60 miles an hour.

What remains of the postal tubes is now lying unused below the streets, but undoubtedly not for long: subterranean space is too rare a commodity in New York. The increasing demand for high-speed Internet access, for instance, has started a new wave of underground activities. There are plans to install fiber optic cables in obsolete water pipes, yet the old pneumatic tubes may be better suited, since they lack the valves that could impede the line's continuity.

Unfortunately, the largest pneumatic tube in the city's history has been entirely dismantled. This tunnel was part of the city's first experimental subway system, built more than a century ago by Alfred Beach.

part II The Subway System

*Figure 7.1 Alfred Beach proposed a pneumatic underground railway
running from the Battery to Harlem*

CHAPTER SEVEN

# The Secret Subway of Alfred Beach

In February 1870, a selected group of New York's most prominent residents received a surprising invitation. A certain Alfred Ely Beach was requesting their presence at the opening of New York City's first subway. Although a newspaper had first mentioned the project three months earlier, the excavations had proceeded without public knowledge. Now the news of its opening quickly became the talk of the town.

Since the mid-nineteenth century, Manhattan had been suffering from a catastrophic transportation problem. Streetcars and carriages were fighting for every inch of space on the larger avenues, while trying to maintain breakneck speeds. A contemporary writer noted that anyone attempting to cross Broadway amidst this madness would be "exceedingly fortunate if they get over with sound bones and a whole skin." When New Yorkers heard that London was opening a subway in 1863, they clamored for their own underground trains, to the point that many of the city's politicians, scientists, and inventors began applying themselves to the problem in earnest.

But the city was in the firm grasp of William "Boss" Tweed. One of the most corrupt politicians in the city's history, Tweed was receiving generous kickbacks from the streetcar business. Whoever wanted to build a subway system first had to substantially line Tweed's pockets, which put most candidates out of the running. They had to get on Tweed's good side in the political realm as well, which proved the stumbling block for the railroad magnate Hugh B. Willson, whose proposal for a subterranean railway from the Battery to Central Park was rejected by Tweed in 1866.

Thus, the city was bowled over by the news of Beach's invention. Beach, a publisher by trade, had turned the struggling *Scientific American* into a successful magazine and was also an established inventor who was looking toward London for inspiration. By 1863, London had built a short pneumatic railway and installed a mail tube system. Beach began to develop his own plans for a pneumatic train that could be blown through a cylinder by means of a large fan.

At the American Institute Fair in 1867 he demonstrated a prototype of the system that actually transported 10 people seated inside a plywood tube from one part of the building to another, accompanied by loud cheers from the audience. Finally, he thought, he had found an answer to the city's nagging transportation problem. Now he only had to somehow get around Boss Tweed, who would most certainly block the project.

Instead of going the official route, Beach decided to build the subway in secret, financed largely with his own money. In 1868 he filed for a permit for the construction of a simple pneumatic mail system under Broadway, which was granted. Next he designed and built a cylindrical tunnel shield—the first such shield in America—which was powered by hydraulic rams and could excavate 17 inches at every thrust. The entrance to his construction site was through the lower basement of Devlin's Clothing Store at the corner of Broadway and Warren Street. It was beyond the walls of this basement that he would start burrowing his tunnel.

With his son Fred and a few other workers, he began his excavations in the sandy underground below the street. So as not to attract attention, the work was done

*Figure 7.2 Beach's workers at the tunneling machine beneath Broadway*

at night, with the soil transported from the store basement into carriages with muffled wheels. Although the working conditions were claustrophobic and dangerous, the tunnel shield proved competent. Even when Beach encountered the remains of an old foundation wall, he was able to force his way through.

But the inventor knew that his largest obstacle remained Boss Tweed. He was hoping to eventually extend the subway route all the way to the Harlem River, which would only be possible if the public's support was overwhelming enough to silence the politician. For this reason, Beach had decided to build only a small segment of the actual train route before focusing his efforts on impressing the public. Below Warren Street he built a waiting room of legendary opulence. Furnished with chandeliers, paintings, a piano, a fountain, and a goldfish tank, the hall resembled the luxurious sitting room of a grand mansion. Velvet curtains covered fake windows to relieve any sense of oppression that might disturb people sensitive to being underground.

The work on the tunnel lasted 58 days. The nine-foot-wide tube spanned only the length of one block, from Warren Street to Murray Street. Beach had constructed an elegant train car with 22 upholstered seats and zircon lights, which could be blown through the tunnel like a sailboat and sucked back to the station at the end of the ride after a signal had been sent through the telegraph wires along the tunnel walls. The large rotary fan, nicknamed "The Western Tornado," was discreetly kept out of sight in the adjacent cellar room.

The opening reception on February 26, 1870, was spectacular. Reporters from the *New York Times,* the *New York Sun, Scientific American,* and other influential publications came and voiced their astonishment and delight. The *New York Herald* wrote that the station was as magical as "Aladdin's cave." For months, New Yorkers let themselves be transported from one end of the tunnel to the other.

Beach received the popular support he wanted, but, as expected, he had made himself a powerful enemy. When Tweed threatened to shut the subway down, the inventor appealed directly to Albany, presenting the Beach Transit Bill for an underground railway whose excavation and operation would not interfere with street traffic. The proposed cost to the city: five million dollars. Tweed countered with an $80 million transit plan for an elevated railway, which despite the high cost would most certainly paralyze traffic during its construction. Tweed's ally, Governor John Hoffman, vetoed the Beach plan and gave the green light to his friend's elevated rails.

Beach kept his showcase open to the public as he continued the battle for his subway, but even after Tweed's corruption was finally exposed in 1871, leading to his removal from office, the inventor was unable to find the necessary funds. Engineers proved skeptical

*Figure 7.3  View from Beach's tunnel into the station, showing the experimental train*

about the powers of pneumatic transport over the proposed distances, and the stock market panic of 1873 was the final blow. Realizing that no one was willing to invest in his project, Beach finally shut down his experimental railway. He died in 1896 without ever having seen the real subway in New York.

The tunnel, however, remained. Through the years, Beach's subway faded into oblivion, until in 1912, when the Degnon Contracting Company was preparing its construction of the subway station at City Hall, an article in the *New York Times* reminded the public about the historic treasure that was about to be uncovered below Broadway. The contractors, who entered the tunnel by candlelight from a ventilation shaft in City Hall Park, did find the tube nearly intact, with the train and tunneling shield still sitting inside. While the wooden train had crumbled on the tracks, the tunnel itself had remained sound. Eventually, however, all the remnants of Beach's tube had to make way for the track areas of City Hall Station.

But what happened to the waiting room? The luxurious station, abandoned beneath the sidewalk, continues to fuel the imagination of many New Yorkers ruminating on the mysteries of the city's underground. Unfortunately its splendor was not long-lived.

In December 1898, the Rogers, Peet & Co. Building, which occupied the corner of Warren Street and Broadway, was destroyed in a blaze that wrecked most of the city block. The building had housed the Devlin's Clothing Store and provided the entrance to Beach's tunnel in its lower basement. During the construction work that followed, the former station was briefly uncovered beneath the sidewalk. It had been walled off from the tunnel and reputedly used as a shooting gallery for some time. In its new, much more prosaic incarnation, it barely attracted attention before disappearing again below the pavement of Warren Street.

*Figure 8.1  Train tracks below midtown Manhattan*

CHAPTER EIGHT

# Welcome to the Subway Crush

Alfred Beach's pneumatic subway was only one of various proposed solutions to New York's traffic problem. In 1867 the inventor Charles Harvey had already introduced the first prototype of an elevated train on Greenwich Street. After Harvey's test run proved successful and the public appeared to embrace the idea of an elevated rail system, William Tweed stepped in to block its development. But here his efforts were unsuccessful. Harvey also had powerful friends in Albany, and after the first line in lower Manhattan opened in 1868, the network quickly expanded. By 1875, elevated trains had reached 42nd Street.

As the system spread across the city, protests began to rise. The steel viaducts darkened the streets, the engines were noisy, and the steam from the locomotives polluted the air. Although many New Yorkers were still afraid of what dangers the underground might hold, Mayor Abram Hewitt was trying to convince the city council to provide funding for a subway. His proposal, later referred to as the Hewitt Formula, entailed that while the city would supply the financing and retain ownership, a private company would oversee the construction and administration of the subway.

In 1891 the Rapid Transit Act was signed, giving the official green light for the subway construction, but years were spent trying to iron out the details of how such a massive project would be funded. Although the reign of Boss Tweed had long been shattered, the public had no faith in city financing and waited instead for a private sponsor to take over. When no one stepped up to the plate by 1894, New Yorkers decided on municipal ownership after all. By 1900 the funds were finally allotted to a private contractor, John B. McDonald, who was to act under the supervision of the engineer William Barclay Parsons.

However, in order to proceed, McDonald had to put up a steep bond to cover the construction risks. Here, August Belmont stepped in. Belmont, who had inherited millions by age 16, had long tried to invest in the subway business, and

*Figure 8.2 The IRT was constructed with both express and local tracks*

when McDonald asked for his assistance, he recognized the great financial potential. Wasting no time, he founded the Rapid Transit Subway Construction Company, which would provide financial backing, and a month later, on March 24, 1900, the official groundbreaking ceremony was held in front of City Hall. In May 1902, Belmont incorporated the agency that would be responsible for operating the subway, the Interborough Rapid Transit Company (IRT).

The first subway line was planned to lead from City Hall north to Grand Central, then turn west below 42nd Street to what is now Times Square, turning north again at Broadway, all the way to the Bronx. Here, the 9.1 mile long subway would connect with the elevated rails.

First, the crucial issue of how deep to build the subway had to be addressed. Parsons, the chief engineer, had been concerned with this question for years and had already conducted test borings in lower Manhattan. He was also familiar with the substantial underground construction experience of European cities such as

*Figure 8.3  Construction of the initial IRT line under Broadway in Midtown*

London, whose subway had been in operation since 1863. Parsons proposed that rather than tunneling deep underground, as in London, the New York subway should follow Budapest by working in an open cut. In Budapest, the excavations had proceeded by means of digging a deep trench, building masonry walls and reinforcing the framework with steel beams. Before the tunnels were roofed over and buried under soil, the tracks were laid and the station interiors were finished underground.

Although this excavation method required the streets to be ripped open, disrupting traffic, Parsons's proposal was adopted. For the next few years the public had to contend with ruptured streets and hellish traffic conditions—even more so than today. Around 10,000 workers excavated a total of more than three million cubic yards of soil and rocks. Underground conduits had to be relocated, building foundations had to be supported and the track beds had to be kept dry, which proved particularly challenging when the tunnels were built through the former Collect Pond.

The subway construction had its share of calamities. The first major accident was caused by the worker Moses Epps in January 1902, when he decided to warm his freezing hands by lighting a candle inside a construction shack on Park Avenue, several blocks south of Grand Central. As he stepped outside for a moment, the candle fell to the ground, igniting a paper bag and setting off more than 500 pounds of dynamite stored in the shack. The explosion killed five people, caused more than 100 injuries, destroyed the Murray Hill Hotel and shattered the clock in the facade of Grand Central Depot. This accident resulted in a tightening of regulations regarding explosive materials in New York.

Worse was a second dynamite-related accident below 195th Street in 1903, when a foreman brought his crew back into the tunnel too soon after a scheduled

*Figure 8.4  The City Hall Station featured vaulted ceilings by Rafael Guastavino*

blast. Not all of the explosives had been detonated, and the remaining dynamite ignited just as the men entered that tunnel segment. The foreman and nine workers died. Others were wedged below boulders, unable to free themselves. By the time the subway opened, 120 men had lost their lives in its construction.

On October 27, 1904, the entire city was swept up by the inauguration ceremonies. There were parties across the city, the streets were decorated with flags, and everyone brought whistles and other noisemakers to celebrate. Inside City Hall Park, thousands of spectators were fighting for a good location from which to witness the official opening, while church bells were ringing and the ships on the Hudson blasted their foghorns.

Before the inaugural ride at City Hall, which was limited to a specially invited party, August Belmont gave a speech and handed the silver control keys to Mayor George B. McClellan. This was only intended as a symbolic gesture; McClellan was supposed to pass the keys to the train operator. But to everyone's surprise, McClellan saw this as an invitation to climb behind the controls himself. At top speed, he took the train from City Hall to 103rd Street, where he finally relinquished his seat.

Between 122nd and 135th streets, the tracks went across an open viaduct, where the subway train could be admired by the public for the first time. Throngs of spectators had climbed the roofs and fire escapes and assembled in the streets to witness the train emerging from the tunnel. The train slowed down and whistled, and the sirens from nearby factories, along with foghorns from the ships, returned the greeting.

More than 150,000 people took the subway on that first day, crowding some of the stations with such enthusiasm that the police had to restrain the masses with force. Crowds gathered around the stations, waiting to experience the strange spectacle of people suddenly emerging from underground. The demand did not die down over the next few days, and on the first Sunday after the opening, the out-of-towners arriving for their first taste of the subway greatly increased the crush.

All at once, the subway had become the ultimate city attraction. New Yorkers would put on nice clothes, dine at a swanky restaurant, and top off the evening by riding a few stops on the subway. Skeptics had proclaimed that "New Yorkers only went underground once, after they died." Physicians warned of the bad air and the eye damage that would result from watching the tunnel columns go by at high speed. Yet the throngs and the fascination only increased. One woman, nicknamed "the Sentinel," had to be dragged home by her husband after continuously watching the trains enter and leave Times Square for four days. Soon there was a hit song called "The Subway Glide" and a dance, "The Subway Express Two Step," in which dancers imitated the shaking of the train. New Yorkers were apparently enamored

*Figure 8.5  City Hall station, now abandoned, was the site of the IRT's inauguration*

with the idea of disappearing down a hole in the street and casually popping up somewhere else, as if it were the most natural thing in the world.

The mysterious subterranean world that was now traversed by powerful engines exerted such an attraction that some intrepid New Yorkers felt compelled to explore it. The first subway explorer to get killed by a train was Leidschnudel Dreispul, who decided to take a walk on the tracks outside of the 137th Street station and was promptly run over. The slow trolleys operating before the subway had not posed a threat to pedestrians; jumping out of the way was such a common pastime that the Brooklyn baseball team had adopted the name "Dodgers." But the IRT moved at a speed of 45 miles an hour, and although the company had posted warnings to stay clear of the tracks, Dreispul was merely the first of many adventurous New Yorkers whose forays into the subway system came to a bad end.

Even before this line had opened, Belmont had planned a second line that would connect Brooklyn to the network in Manhattan. The construction began in

1905 and involved building the first subway tunnel below the East River, which became the scene of one of the most unusual events in subway construction history.

As was customary in subaquatic tunnels, the air pressure had been raised to keep out the water, and one day there was a blowout in the tunnel ceiling. The sandhog Richard Creedon tried to plug a leak that had developed near the rim of the tunneling shield, but the hole suddenly widened to four feet. Creedon was caught up in the stream, sucked through the hole in the tunnel, and catapulted through 27 feet of riverbed and water. Miraculously, he survived. He was propelled through the silt and water with such force that he popped up in a tall geyser on the river and after being rescued only felt somewhat dazed. After being administered plentiful libations by a surgeon, he went home, put on his party clothes and held a reception, where he told his befuddled visitors that his journey had been no big deal. "I was flying through the air," he told a reporter, "and before I comes down, I had a fine view of the city."

When the two tunnel halves from Brooklyn and Manhattan were ready to be joined below the East River, the crew in the Brooklyn end decided to pay homage to this incident. They plotted to break through the remaining wall by means of Creedon's body—at the suggestion of Creedon himself. He stood in front of the partition while the workers pointed the compressed air nozzle at the ground near

*Figure 8.6  The Mineola, August Belmont's private car, can now be seen at the Shore Line Trolley Museum*

him, until a small hole formed in the wall. "Here, give it to me in the back," Creedon called and turned his back to the men, who now trained the air stream directly on him. Promptly he was shot through the partition while everyone cheered, much to the surprise of the crew on the other side. Being blown through a tunnel must be an addictive experience. Don't try it at home.

While August Belmont saw to it that the subway system expanded at a steady pace, he liked to play as well, albeit on a much more elaborate scale. In order to soften the habitual journeys to his racetrack on Long Island, he had a small train built for himself—the Mineola, the only private train in the history of the New York subway. "Minnie was a lady," it is said to this day. The car was truly a work of luxury, with mahogany walls and a kitchen well stocked with champagne and gourmet food. From its 12 leather chairs, his occasional dinner guests could admire the subway tunnels through the large windows. Whenever Belmont felt like traveling from the Belmont Hotel at Park Avenue and 42nd Street to Long Island, he had the Mineola brought from its private spur onto the regular IRT tracks, where he could enter it from a door in his subterranean bar. After Belmont's death and a period of collecting dust in several layup yards around the city, the Mineola was brought to the Shore Line Trolley Museum in Connecticut, where it can be visited today.

## COMPETITION IN THE UNDERGROUND

Soon the subway was filled beyond capacity; by 1905 the trains already had to transport twice as many passengers per mile as in the London Underground. Yet despite the continuing increase in riders, Belmont was not interested in building a second line. To him, any train that was not filled to the bursting point was a waste of money. At the same time he acted swiftly to eliminate any potential competition, such as another line proposed by the Rapid Transit Commission.

Only when the Brooklyn Rapid Transit Company (BRT) decided to expand in 1911 did Belmont's reign over the subway come to an end. The BRT, which controlled elevated lines and trolleys in Brooklyn, proposed a second line that would connect its system to Manhattan. By this time, the city was eager to undermine Belmont's monopoly and supported the BRT's project. In March 1913, the contracts for a dual system were signed.

Soon after, the network took on gigantic proportions. In 1920 it had reached a total of 202 miles, whereas the subways in London only had 156 miles and Paris only 59 miles of tracks. It was extraordinary that two systems were in competition in the same city, and while it fueled the growth of both enterprises, this was not necessarily to the benefit of the customers (such as when two lines would run

*Figure 8.7  Subway service between Manhattan and Brooklyn began in 1908*

parallel to each other without offering any transfer points). Nonetheless, the dual system managed to unite the entire city. Now that there were connections from the Bronx to Brooklyn, New York could expand horizontally and vertically at the same time. Building high-rises only made sense if there were masses of people to fill them. By providing an efficient means to bring people from outlying residential areas to work in Manhattan, the subway gave rise to an increasing profusion of skyscrapers.

The BRT, however, turned out to be ill-fated. On November 1, 1918, the company's train operators went on strike, which inadvertently resulted in the worst subway accident in New York history to date. Because of the strike, the line from Park Row in Manhattan to Coney Island was operated by employees who were not qualified to conduct trains. Anthony Luciano, a conductor with only limited experience, was assigned to the Brighton Line.

Soon after he took the controls of the train, he missed a turn and had to reverse to switch tracks. Luciano got back on route, but had lost time, and to make up for it he began speeding toward Prospect Park in Brooklyn, passing the Consumers Park Station without stopping. Whether his brakes really failed, as he later claimed in court, could not be determined conclusively, but when he barged into the tunnel at Malbone Street, the train was going at a speed of 30 to 40 miles an hour. Because of a sharp turn in the line, the top speed for this tunnel was only six miles an hour. The train could not take the curve and derailed.

The results were horrendous. Several cars slammed into the steel beams, slicing passengers to pieces. Although the noise of the crash could be heard a mile away, it took more than a half hour for any rescuers to arrive at the wreck. The spectators

*Figure 8.8  The site of the Malbone Street accident today*

at the edge of the tunnel were shocked to see the first survivor appear from the darkness. Covered in blood, he was wearing barely more than a shirt and one shoe. Because so much of the train had compacted into a big pile, the victims could be recovered only with great difficulty. There were 97 deaths and more than 100 injuries.

Astonishingly, Luciano had not only survived, but had somehow left the accident site and gone home. He was arrested the same night, but it was the officers of the BRT who had assigned Luciano to the job who were ultimately held responsible for the accident. By the time the trial ended several years later, the BRT was bankrupt. In 1923 the company was restructured under the name Brooklyn-Manhattan Transit Corporation (BMT). The public's association of Malbone Street with the accident was so strong that it was renamed Empire Boulevard.

John F. Hylan, who was mayor from 1918 to 1925, was an outspoken opponent of the private ownership of the city's subway, which he considered detrimental to public interest. In 1924, his proposal for New York's third subway line, owned and

*Figure 8.9  Inside the IRT Substation 13 on 53rd Street*

operated by a newly formed Board of Transportation was adopted. The Independent Subway System (IND) focused on transferring the remaining elevated lines into the underground and improving transportation in the older parts of the city. For the first time, New York was building a subway line that did not considerably add to an expansion of the visible cityscape. Yet, never again would the subways have such power. As of the 1930s, it was Robert Moses, the supreme and highly unpopular champion of automobile traffic, whose transportation decisions changed the shape of the city.

The three separate subway lines were finally united by Mayor Fiorello LaGuardia in 1940. The unification of these privately held enterprises was a massive undertaking. By now there were 293 miles of tracks and almost 35,000 employees. To this day, the New York City Subway Authority, the agency created to supervise the unified subway, belongs to the Metropolitan Transit Authority (MTA). As of 2004, the MTA's subway system includes 685 miles of passenger service tracks and 490 stations, serving more than four million passengers a day. Even now, the system is continually under construction, and large projects, such as the extension of the 7 line into Manhattan's west side and the completion of the Second Avenue subway, loom on the horizon.

## THE SECOND AVENUE SUBWAY

Up until a few years ago, the unfinished tunnels of the Second Avenue line were a refuge for homeless people and drug addicts. The three sections that have already been completed are sealed, waiting for work on the line to be resumed. Plans for the Second Avenue subway have been around since the 1920s, yet its tunnels have never seen a train.

Although the first plans were presented in 1927 to relieve the congestion of the IRT line beneath Lexington Avenue, and the construction of new tunnels from the Lower East Side to Harlem was approved two years later, the Great Depression threw a wrench into the schedule. It was not until 1944 that new plans were drafted, which included connections to the Manhattan and Williamsburg bridges and to the Sixth Avenue line at Central Park. Yet, for political and financial reasons, the project was delayed again. In the meantime, the increasing construction of high-rises on the East Side brought the Lexington Avenue line of the subway to the bursting point.

In 1967, Governor Nelson Rockefeller again allocated funding for the project, but only three segments were excavated before budget problems halted the construction in 1975, just after the groundbreaking ceremonies on a fourth section

*Figure 8.10  Knife switches inside Substation 13*

in the East Village. By then, the city's subway system had become vastly unpopular; it was considered unreliable and dangerous, and the MTA turned much of its attention to the eradication of graffiti, which to many people was symbolic of the deterioration of New York City. The Second Avenue project was pushed to the back burner, and in the 1980s, the MTA considered renting out the unfinished tunnels as clubs or wine cellars. Only in the late 1990s, especially during the mayoral election in 2001, did the project again get public attention. The MTA is planning to revive the construction in the near future.

*Figure 9.1  The abandoned station at 91st Street was part of the first IRT line*

# CHAPTER NINE

# Ghost Stations

Taking a subway through Berlin before East and West Germany were reunified in 1990 could have been an eerie experience. The train from the west would barrel through sections of communist East Berlin without stopping, passing all the stations that had been sealed to prevent the oppressed residents escaping onto a subway into freedom. As seen from the trains, the abandoned stations seemed like tombs; what was once a bustling stop had been smothered into silence. Behind the barricaded doors lay mysterious, forbidden things that no one could access without risking their lives.

The fascination with ghost stations is prevalent in Europe, where there is a host of books on the subject, particularly about the nearly 40 abandoned stops of the London Underground. No wonder then, that underground tourists come to New York, one of the world's largest subway systems, expecting to admire an entertaining variety of buried platforms from passing trains. Whether in books like *The Mole People* or movies such as *Mimic*, the fantasy of ornate, ghostly stations slumbering deep in the underground has been widely perpetuated. The reality, however, is far more prosaic.

Manhattan's subway network contains only four stations that have been closed in their entirety, not including those that were affected by the terror attacks on 9/11. All of these belonged to the first line of the IRT and became obsolete as a result of an elongation of the trains. The IRT's original platforms were designed for only five subway cars. In 1956, the New York Transit Authority began extending the oldest stations to accommodate trains with up to 10 cars.

Four of the stations were bypassed by the reconstruction. The platforms at Worth Street, 18th Street, and 91st Street were already very close to other subway stops, and it did not make sense to upgrade them for continued service. All three of these stations still lie underground, entirely covered with graffiti, and although they can't be visited by the public, their remnants can be viewed in passing from the local trains on the original IRT line.

*Figure 9.2  City Hall station, closed since 1945, still retains some of its former splendor*

The fourth station is widely regarded as the crown jewel of the system. The original City Hall station, the first to be used when the subway was inaugurated in 1904, may win the prize as the underground area that New Yorkers would like to visit the most. Designated a historic landmark, it is the most elegant station in the subway system even today. Colorful tiles and chandeliers contribute to its allure and the vaulted ceilings, designed by the architect Rafael Guastavino, are classic. Three leaded glass windows in the self-supporting roof once allowed daylight to enter the station. Blackened during World War II to prevent attacks, the windows still lie in City Hall Park.

Since the station is inside a loop, it was impractical to extend the platforms. The area was also serviced by the City Hall station of the BMT line and the more popular Brooklyn Bridge station of the IRT, making the original City Hall terminal obsolete by 1945. Throughout the years there have been proposals to turn it into a branch of the Transit Museum, and until the 1990s there were occasional public tours. But because of security concerns—the loop lies almost directly under City Hall—the museum plans were scrapped, the entrances were sealed, and a police booth was installed on the platform. Today the loop is still used to turn around the trains of the 6 line and occasionally the train operators will allow curious passengers to stay on and view the station in passing.

*Figure 9.3  A sealed staircase on the lower level of the BMT City Hall station*

Numerous other stations in the system, such as at Times Square, Chambers Street, and Bergen Street have closed levels and platforms that are rarely seen by anyone outside of transit workers and graffiti writers. One of these stations has become my personal favorite in the entire system. The City Hall station on the BMT line—less glamorous but more intriguing than its IRT sister—has a lower level that was never put into service. Yet the platforms have been maintained, are well illuminated, and serve as a layup and storage area for the MTA. The decrepit shell of an old control tower still sits at its northern end, and the walls and sealed staircases on this level provide a rare chance to see old-school graffiti by legends such as Iz and Min One.

The south end of the station, where the line snakes around the foundation of the Woolworth Building toward Cortlandt Street, is unlike any other spot in the New York underground. The partial construction of this lower level has created a catacomb-like area below the active tracks. Down here, the track beds were never equipped with rails. Instead, groundwater has seeped in to create a small labyrinth of canals, interspersed with narrow maintenance sections. At its far end, the ceiling of the innermost track bed gradually lowers until only a small, wet cavern remains. This is where the northbound train enters the active City Hall platform above, and standing here while a train roars past only a few feet higher is one way to have an earthquake-like experience in New York.

This catacomb section, illumined by occasional yellow lights and strangely without graffiti, is dazzling. The track beds have a few raised sections, creating a striped effect across the deeper flooded areas, which are covered with a white layer of dust. Carl Vincent, an MTA employee who has come here over many years, tells me that this is World Trade Center residue that seeped in from the adjacent Cortlandt Street station. No one ever goes into these catacombs, apparently, and the dust has been left to form ghostly patterns on the water surface, reflecting blue light from a laid-up train ahead.

Two other abandoned subway stations, both in Brooklyn, are notable for having become exhibition sites. The former Court Street stop has been reconstructed into the Transit Museum, and the Myrtle Avenue station has become the site of a large mural by Bill Blass called the *Masstransiscope*, which functions as a zoetrope when seen from the passing trains.

*Figure 9.4  Groundwater has seeped into the unfinished trackbeds of the City Hall station's lower level*

*Figure 9.5  Remnants of the obsolete trolley station at Essex and Delancey streets*

There is also an abandoned station for trolleys in the city's underground. It lies on the Manhattan side of the Williamsburg Bridge, which was opened in 1903 and equipped with several tracks for trains and trolleys. A terminal with eight loops was built at the intersection of Essex and Delancey streets and opened to passengers in 1904. When trolley service was eliminated in 1948, most of the tracks on the bridge made way for traffic lanes. The old station remained underground; some of its remnants can be seen from the platforms of the J, M, and Z lines. The recent renovations of the subway stop did not touch its decrepit structures. The old control tower with its broken windows still keeps watch over the tracks. It may lie undisturbed for some time to come—just another of the inconspicuous ruins of underground New York.

*Figure 10.1 Approaching a laid-up train beneath Broadway*

CHAPTER TEN
# Silent Tunnels

In addition to the closed stations, New York's subway system usually has a few tunnels that are at least temporarily abandoned. They might be the track areas leading to closed platforms or passages that were discontinued shortly after construction, such as the Chrystie Street connection below the Bowery. Passing through, these zones may appear completely dead. Yet any of those tracks can always be put back into service temporarily, either to lay up trains or reroute a line during an emergency. Only those areas without a third rail are truly unused.

The unfinished section of the Second Avenue subway at the Manhattan Bridge, has never seen any tracks, much less a train. When this segment was built in 1975, its excavation partially weakened three support columns of the Confucius Plaza apartments along with the foundation of the bridge's Canal Street entrance. To prevent any additional damage, the MTA has continued maintaining the short tunnel, monitoring it for leaks, rust, and other deterioration. Despite its apparent inaccessibility, this section along the Bowery, which underpins the subway tracks across the bridge, was once a preferred area for the homeless, but in recent years, the MTA has reinforced the locks and alarms to keep out stray visitors.

For some time, a large abandoned track area just above this empty structure was keeping the MTA's unwanted busy nonetheless. When repairs on the Manhattan Bridge shut down this segment of the system during the 1990s, the surrounding tunnels turned into a strange ghost region below Chinatown.

Since they had been put into service, the bridge's north set of tracks were used much more heavily than the south, which led to considerable damage in the structural integrity of the overpass. During a large part of the repair work, the two tracks on its south side were closed. In Manhattan, these tracks led to a section of the Canal Street station that was likewise closed during the construction. Adding to this, two obsolete tracks from the Chambers Street station dead-ended near

*Figure 10.2  A temporarily disused track below Chinatown*

the bridge, and another pair of unused tracks from the abandoned lower level of the BMT City Hall station lay just beyond the Canal Street platforms. Altogether, this could make for a confusing journey beneath Chinatown.

For those of us with a penchant for tunnels, this underground area was irresistible. Walking a dead track from the bridge into the bowels of Manhattan led into a surreal environment. While the rail areas were in shambles, the tunnels' bright lights imparted a constant state of tension and expectancy. Large vacant track and maintenance spaces separated this section from the active subway lines crossing the bridge. They muffled the noise of the approaching trains and otherwise lay in a silence that only emphasized the humming electricity. A few people had pitched camps in the unused worker rooms, but most of the chambers were desolate, containing only shelves and tool chests covered in soot, to all appearances having been untouched for a long time.

Amidst all this desolation, it was the graffiti that brought the area to life, a reminder that you were not on some post-apocalyptic archaeological dig, but in the heart of New York City. *I'M FUCKIN ALIVE* is the name of Revs's book, which consists of a series of autobiographical pages written on the walls of subway tunnels, and it was down here that I first encountered them. On large, light-colored

*The interior of the High Bridge*

Rappelling into one of the piers of the High Bridge.

*Long abandoned, the Croton Aqueduct is being reclaimed by nature*

*Inside a gate chamber of the Croton Aqueduct in the Bronx*

*Looking down the rusted iron water pipe in the High Bridge*

*A catwalk runs along the obsolete water conduit inside the High Bridge*

*A voyage under Manhattan in the "Croton Maid Jr."*

*Two obsolete pipes lead to what was once a storage tank at the top of the High Bridge Water Tower*

*The main steam tunnel of the Pratt Institute*

*The utility cellar of the IRT substation on 53th Street*

*Figure 10.3  Tunnels on the west side of the Manhattan Bridge*

panels, he would write dated entries on subjects ranging from childhood episodes to personal commentaries. No graffiti writer had ever used the medium to tell his own life story, let alone make a point of laying it all on the line. "I wanted it to be as honest as I can make it," he says. "I just wanted it to be straight out, 100 percent the truth on those walls." Initially, he planned to write a page in every subway tunnel in the city; 235 were finished before he was arrested in 2000.

Famous in the 1990s for his street missions with Cost, Revs moved underground after his partner's arrest in 1995, both to avoid getting caught and because he thinks of tunnels as more permanent than the surfaces on the street. Two or three times a week he would descend into the subway, sometimes alone, carrying a custom-made ladder, a roller, and a five-gallon bucket of paint. He would set the ladder in the middle of the tracks or on the wood cover of the third rail, watching for trains as he wrote, and when he saw approaching headlights, he quickly stashed the ladder and stepped aside. He has accidentally stepped on a third rail, not the protective wood cover, but the electrified metal, and is alive to tell the story only because his other foot didn't hit a track. Other such hair-raising experiences include dodging blue sparks from passing wheels, and, after being spotted by the motorman, being chased down a tunnel by a money train. He has also had occasional encounters with underground residents.

One day, wearing an MTA vest, he went to paint a page off a station in Brooklyn. It was a tube tunnel with no clearance, and he ran from the platform to a small maintenance area next to the tracks. He climbed up on a ledge without realizing that someone was sleeping in an alcove directly above him. "I was doing my painting right below him — I didn't even know he was there," Revs recounts. "He says to me, 'Hey, you're MTA?' I said yeah. He starts muttering to himself for a few minutes. Then he goes, 'You're not MTA!' He starts screaming at the top of his lungs. He's yelling: 'Get the fuck out of here!' I told him to just relax himself. I was like, this guy is gonna get me busted. He picked up a broomstick like he was gonna fucking charge me. But for him to get to me, he would have had to slide down this pipe, and he didn't. We just had words. So I finished up what I had to do and then left."

Confrontations like this only happened occasionally and the more usual solitude made the tunnels all the more attractive to him. He also appreciates how drastically different the environment is from the city above. It was his friend Soup who compared going into the subway tunnels to entering a black and white movie. "I thought, he's right. It's a black and white experience."

It really is a black and white experience to walk through the unused subway tunnel that lies 10 stories below Central Park. The bare and relatively modern tunnel walls are sparsely illumined, and the initial segment is conspicuously bare of graffiti. Aside from occasional red signal lights — facing in both directions on the same track — there is no color here at all.

This tunnel begins at the 57th Street station on the Broadway line, a busy track area that includes a short virginal stretch of rails just north of the platforms. The obsolete stub, on the west side of this huge underground space, was once intended to connect to the Eighth Avenue line. Never having been equipped with a third rail, it now dead-ends against a freshly built maintenance shack. Just beyond the shack lies a worker area with a trash-filled emergency hatch that may well contain the largest concentration of squealing rats in the subway system — an appropriate departure point for a tunnel journey that leads beneath the Central Park Zoo.

The Central Park tunnel was constructed to connect with the planned Second Avenue line before heading below the East River to Queens. Excavated in the 1970s with a height of 45 feet, it runs in two arcs — one from Seventh Avenue, the other from Sixth Avenue — to the Lexington Avenue station on the F line on the level of 63rd Street. Because the Second Avenue project never materialized, it was not equipped with track until much after the initial excavation, and its Seventh Avenue segment has never been in regular service. This tunnel is only used to lay up trains at Lexington Avenue.

*Figure 10.4  This tunnel beneath Central Park is currently used only for layups*

*Figure 10.5  A virginal track segment that was intended to connect from the 57th Street station (BMT) to Eighth Avenue*

The lack of trains makes it a very quiet section of the system, and yet, perhaps because of its modern construction, it does not have an abandoned feel to it. Once in a while a solitary Smith/Sane tag breaks the monotony of the tunnel walls. ("That was one of our favorite places to explore since they got rooms all over the place," Smith has mentioned.)

Below Central Park at the level of Seventh Avenue, after the tunnel has turned east under 63rd Street, comes a section where water drizzles from the tunnel ceiling, although up to six feet of concrete were pumped between the steel supports and the schist above to keep out groundwater. Perhaps the underground shower is an inadvertent drain from the pond in the park? Further on, near a legendary stairwell whose signs indicate a total depth of 10 stories, an explosion of graffiti begins. At this point the tracks from the F line run in a parallel tunnel, connected to this one by cutouts and, in the hatch area, a series of empty worker rooms.

Like this one, the F tunnel runs on two levels, the Manhattan-bound tracks on top of the Queens-bound tunnel. Hence the platforms of the next station on

*Figure 10.6  Facing east below 63rd Street: the unused Lexington Avenue platform on the left, the active station on the F line on the right*

*Figure 10.7  This newer Lexington Avenue platform will some day be part
of the Second Avenue subway line*

the F line, Lexington Avenue, are stacked on top of each other and only occupy one side of the tunnel. That is because the other side, beyond the orange-tiled wall, contains a mirror image of this station. But the platform areas on this other side, which the Central Park tunnel emerges into, are still waiting to be finished, as part of the Second Avenue line construction. Here the dividing wall lacks the snazzy orange tile; it is obviously a good step away from being functional. Even the large public stairwell of this deep station, containing a series of escalators, has a ghostly mirror image here. Except that there are no escalators, just a large, unfinished cavern with long staircases.

Walking in this unused area, it is possible to hear the voices of the subway passengers on the other side of the wall. I have stood there myself, waiting for a train, not realizing that a whole other world lay just beyond the orange tiles, and that some day I would end up in this unusual subterranean area, after a pleasant stroll far beneath Central Park.

*Figure 10.8  Ghostly staircases at the eastern end of the Lexington Avenue station*

part III Trains into New York

*Figure 11.1 The McAdoo tunnels, which opened in 1908, are now used by PATH trains*

# CHAPTER ELEVEN

# Moving Trains Below the Hudson

During the railroad age in the mid-nineteenth century, New York City, by now a thriving metropolis, found itself at a disadvantage in connecting with the rest of the country. Cutting the city off from any direct link to the west was the Hudson River, which, in the vicinity of lower Manhattan, was considered much too wide for a bridge. This meant that trains either had to enter the city from the north, or stop at the New Jersey shore, where passengers and freight had to be transferred onto ferries and barges. Since the locomotives were still powered by steam, a subaquatic tunnel was considered problematic as well. Never mind the difficulties of such a construction itself, without an expensive and complicated ventilation system, there was the danger of suffocating everyone on such a long journey. Unfortunately, the first person who set out to overcome these obstacles met with disastrous results.

Colonel DeWitt Haskins, a railroad engineer with a keen interest in recent tunneling developments, decided to build a tube from 15th Street in Jersey City to lower Manhattan. After he had secured financing and founded the Hudson Tunnel Railroad Company, he initiated the construction of two single-tracked tubes, starting on the north tunnel first.

The construction began in 1874, not long after work had started on the Brooklyn Bridge, and both projects shared one important factor: the crews were laboring under water with the aid of compressed air. In both cases, this entailed working inside a confined space, in which the air pressure had been raised so high that its ceiling could carry the weight of all the water above. Both sets of engineers were closely following the work of James Buchanan Eads, who had sunk the first caisson for the world's first steel bridge across the Mississippi in 1869. The Brooklyn Bridge and Haskins's tunnel were the East Coast's first experiments with compressed air, and soon New York would learn to dread a new ailment: caisson disease, also known as "the bends."

*Figure 11.2 The excavation shield used for the McAdoo tubes below the Hudson*

Working with compressed air required the use of an airlock, a narrow chamber with two doors, which had been invented by a British engineer in the 1830s. Once a few workers had entered the chamber and the pressure was raised, the second door would open and admit the men into the underwater space. The compressed air, at the very least, inflicted superficial physical changes. Men spoke in high-pitched voices, had trouble breathing, and complained of ringing ears.

But more serious symptoms were soon reported, followed by fatalities. On unpredictable occasions, the change in pressure could result in temporary paralysis and excruciating pain, causing some of the afflicted to double up like a jackknife. The first death from the bends in New York came in 1872, when a worker named John Myers exited a caisson of the Brooklyn Bridge after his first day on the job and was felled by the decompression process. There were 28 severe cases of the bends during the bridge job, three of which were fatal. Soon thereafter, four men would die from decompression disease inside the East River Gas Tunnel. Although some lessons were learned—no one died of the bends while the Williamsburg Bridge was built from 1897 to 1903—underwater construction projects in New York would continue to claim lives.

In the case of Haskins's tunnel, the airlock led from an entrance chamber into the north tube, an iron shell that was bolted together plate by plate and then

*Figure 11.3 The meeting point of the two tunnel segments below the river*

reinforced internally by bricks. Although an injunction had delayed the work for several years, the construction itself proceeded quickly. Together, the miners, welders, masons, and laborers extended the tube into the river at a rate of five feet per day.

On July 21, 1880, a new shift had just entered the airlock when a leak formed in the tunnel's roof. The roof collapsed and the door between the airlock and connecting chamber was wedged shut. The eight men inside the airlock, who could see the obstruction from the door's porthole window, decided to get out, although 20 men were still in the connecting chamber. They broke the window inside the exit door of the airlock, stabilizing the pressure until the door opened and they could run out. This meant that the airlock filled with silt and water, trapping the other men at the head of the tunnel. The 20 workers drowned.

It took three months and a new airlock until the connecting chamber could finally be cleared out and the bodies retrieved. Nonetheless, work continued at a quick pace and the south tube was started. In addition to the roughly 40 men extending the tunnels, a horse and mule were taken through the airlock and now lived inside the tubes. A contemporary writer reported that at the end, while the horse did not survive decompression, the mule was "liberally dosed with ergot, whiskey, and ginger," and passed back out through the airlock in good spirits. When a lack of funds resulting from the tragic accident halted all work in November 1882,

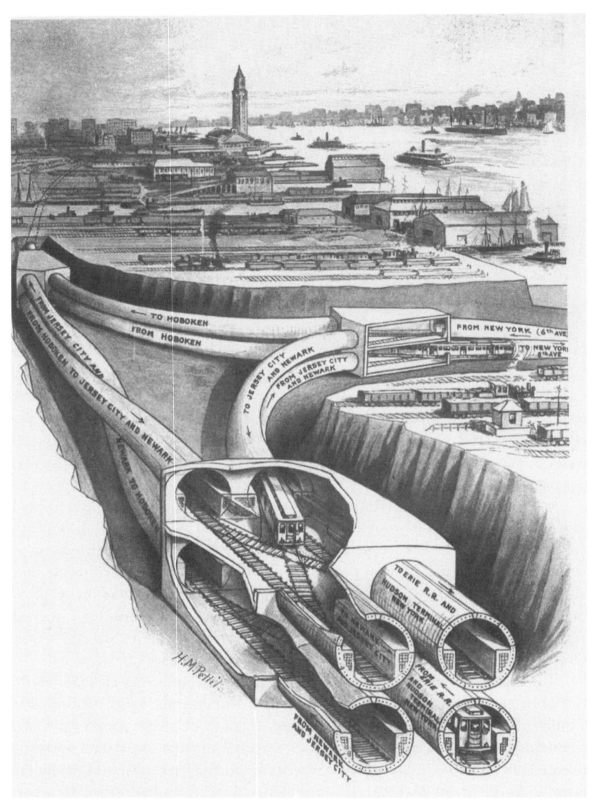

*Figure 11.4  A cross section of the PATH tunnels under Jersey City.*

1,550 feet had been built of the north tube and 570 feet of the south. Both segments were abandoned.

William McAdoo, an attorney who had moved to New York from Tennessee in 1892, was also interested in tunneling under the Hudson. Having worked on the electrified Knoxville Street Railroad in his home state, he believed that powering the locomotives with electricity rather than steam was the solution to the problem posed by the river. McAdoo was excited to hear about Haskins's abandoned experiment and entered a partnership with John Dos Passos, the former director of the now obsolete Hudson Tunnel Railroad Company (and father of the author of the same name).

As president of the newly formed Hudson and Manhattan Railroad Company (H&M), McAdoo arranged to continue work on the larger abandoned tube, creating an entirely new section to serve as the south tube while Haskins's other original tunnel segment was left obsolete. In 1902 the first excavations were underway, and on March 11, 1904, workers connected the first two tunnel halves coming from New Jersey and Manhattan. Soon, work on another pair of tunnels began, linking Exchange Place in New Jersey with Cortlandt Street in Manhattan. Here the H&M built the underground Hudson Terminal and topped it off with a 22-story office building with two towers. In the meantime, additional stations

*Figure 11.5 McAdoo preferred to design his stations with elegantly vaulted ceilings*

in New York and New Jersey had been finished, extending the line on both sides of the Hudson.

McAdoo not only supervised the construction and design of the tunnels but also personally took care of advertising his new system. On the morning before the H&M line's official opening in February 1908, the first train departed from Manhattan to Hoboken with a special "tunnel edition" of the *Jersey City Journal* aboard. The opening was celebrated with great ceremony. When the invited guests assembled inside the 19th Street station, they had to wait in complete darkness, until an employee telegraphed to Washington, whereupon President Theodore Roosevelt pressed a button from the White House and activated the station's electricity. After this dramatic initiation, the maiden voyage was begun with much cheer. At the state line—halfway below the Hudson—the governors of New Jersey and New York shook hands.

The *New York Times* praised the tunnels as "one of the greatest engineering feats ever accomplished, greater perhaps than the Panama Canal will be when opened."

*Figure 11.6 The Hudson Terminal in lower Manhattan was demolished to make way for the World Trade Center*

With his personal attention to safety and comfort, embodied by the slogan "The public be pleased," William McAdoo endeared himself to his employees and passengers alike, making the line tremendously popular. The downtown pair of tunnels were opened the following year, and after entering a partnership with the Pennsylvania Railroad, the H&M offered service between the Hudson Terminal and Newark by 1911. McAdoo had also provided convenient transfer points between the main terminals in Manhattan and the subway system.

After World War II, the H&M, like most other rail companies, was in dire financial shape. Any previously proposed expansion plans did not materialize. As of a few years ago, the tunneling shield and other equipment were still sitting in an enormous maintenance chamber outside of the 9th Street station, just as they had been left in the early twentieth century. In the 1960s the nearly bankrupt company was taken over by the New York Port Authority, which continued the line under a new name, Port Authority Trans Hudson (PATH). Acquiring the Hudson Terminal on Cortlandt Street was an important motive for the purchase. On the site of this station, the Port Authority was planning another momentous project—the construction of the World Trade Center.

*Figure 12.1  Precarious excavations for the Pennsy tunnels along 33rd Street*

# CHAPTER TWELVE

# The Rise and Fall of Penn Station

The largest and most powerful railroad in the country at the end of the nineteenth century was the Pennsylvania Railroad (PRR). The inconvenience posed by the Hudson River was all the more annoying to the "Pennsy"—as it was affectionately known—because its main competitor, the New York Central, was able to run passenger and freight trains directly into the city from the north, whereas it still had to rely on ferries.

Alexander Cassatt, the company's president, had been following the railroad experiments with electrification in Europe with great interest, and after attending the inauguration of the first train station for electric trains in Paris in 1901, he decided to replace his railroad's steam locomotives. By the end of that year, Cassatt announced that the Pennsylvania Railroad would build tunnels beneath both the Hudson and the East Rivers, and connect New York and Long Island to the mainland via a grandiose station in midtown Manhattan. In anticipation of this move, he had already bought the Long Island Rail Road for the PRR during the previous year.

The first of the tunnels beneath the Hudson River was completed by November 1906, waiting to be reinforced by a series of immense concrete columns, which supported the tubes in the bedrock beneath. The tunnels to Long Island did not lag far behind. When the two halves were about to meet beneath the East River, the workers pushed a pipe through the remaining barrier to communicate and check the alignment. Noticing that the air pressure in both halves was slightly different, they began sending things to each other through the pipe, such as a toy train, which thus became the first train to traverse this East River tunnel. The train was followed by a doll, the "first lady" of the tunnel, which was later presented to the chief engineers as a souvenir.

After a promising start, the excavations through Manhattan toward the planned terminal by means of a tunneling shield had to be stopped when the workers came across quicksand and an underground stream on 33rd Street between Madison and Seventh Avenue. Before it had been buried beneath the streets, the stream had originated at Times Square, flowing down Broadway to the vicinity of 34th Street and then turning sharply toward the East River. Near Lexington Avenue it expanded into what was once called Sunfish Pond.

The problem with excavating through a buried stream was that it effectively created a drain for the water, thus causing the surrounding soil to settle and building foundations to sink. The contractors experienced this firsthand in December 1906, when a truck plunged through the pavement on 33rd Street because the subsurface soil had washed away. To navigate the subterranean waters, the contractors had to tear up the streets and continue tunneling by means of the cut and cover method, which they first needed to get permits for. This entailed not only an unwelcome delay but the animosity of nearby residents, who were worried that their houses — like the truck — would be swallowed by the underground.

In the meantime, the excavations for a colossal edifice had started in midtown Manhattan, creating a vast and conspicuous hole 58 feet deep. The architect Charles McKim was modeling the steel and glass design of Pennsylvania Station on the Crystal Palace, which had briefly occupied the site of today's Bryant Park before burning down in 1856. The design of the station's interior, in contrast, was inspired by the ornate Caracalla Baths in Rome. The completed station was stunning. Its Corinthian columns were six stories tall and its vaulted ceilings, frequently compared

*Figure 12.2 Pennsylvania Station was a lavish monument to the railroad age*

to St. Peter's Basilica in Rome, were highly detailed. It seemed as momentous and eternal as the structures erected in antiquity.

During the inauguration on November 27, 1910, more than 100,000 people streamed into the building to admire its palatial halls. The Pennsy's arrival in New York was nothing short of triumphant. At the height of its success in 1936, Penn Station serviced 176 million visitors, but a decade later, as rail travel was increasingly replaced by cars and airplanes, the passenger count began to plunge. By 1951, the Pennsy's finances were deeply in the red, and there were no funds to maintain the station. At last the railroad company decided to sell the air rights above the station area, which meant that the building itself had to go.

*Figure 12.3  Penn Station's original concourse*

In October 1963, in an act of vandalism that lives in infamy to this day, Penn Station was felled. Only when the building had been reduced to a massive heap of rubble did most New Yorkers realize what they had just lost. The present structure, which combines LIRR, Amtrak, and subway services in a garishly bright labyrinth below Madison Square Garden, has all the charm of a neo-Stalinist shopping mall. Almost nothing of the old structure is left. Perhaps Penn Station will reacquire a semblance of its former grandeur, if the plans to move the train service into the historic post office building across the street on Eighth Avenue work out.

Not only has the proposal for the station's impending move made the news in recent years, but the state of some of Amtrak's emergency exits and connecting tunnels has also come under public scrutiny. After the catastrophic tunnel fire in Kaprun, Austria, in November 2000, the renewed attention on emergency escape routes in New York showed that some of Amtrak's tunnel exits contained spiral staircases 10 stories high and so narrow that each step could only accommodate one person at a time.

*Figure 12.4  Tracks leading west out of Penn Station.*

*Figure 12.5  A recently sealed hatch leading to Amtrak tunnels in Queens*

The emergency exit leading to a hatch in Queens that I visited with my friends Joe and Aaron before 9/11 seemed to be in good shape and used rather frequently, though not for its intended purpose. We descended a series of rungs three stories deep into what was once a maintenance area next to an active Amtrak tunnel, where the trains dipped beneath the East River at high speeds on their way to Penn Station. There were two small rooms, one of which contained a grate through which we could see into the tunnel. Not far from us was another maintenance area from which a radio was blaring; someone seemed to be living there. Our area also showed traces of habitation — trash, needles, old clothes, and porn magazines.

In December 2002, Amtrak awarded a contract to Granite Construction for the demolition and reconstruction of the emergency exits and shafts in the area we visited that day. A new structure will be built near the head of the tunnels to house wider staircases, ventilation units, and power substations. The construction is expected to be finished in 2006.

*Figure 13.1  The anatomy of Grand Central Terminal*

# CHAPTER THIRTEEN

# The Mysteries of Grand Central

It was with great interest that I read about a rumored connection between Grand Central Terminal and the Waldorf-Astoria Hotel in the late 1990s. Apparently the historic station did not just have the layup yards, track spurs, and maintenance areas that would be expected in the world's largest train station. Rather, it seemed that these immense catacombs also contained the partial manifestations of a multitude of plans, private wishes, and failed intentions. Its functions went well beyond mere train service to touch on other, vastly different realms of life in New York, such as, in this case, one politician's request to keep his wheelchair use out of the public eye. The private connection to the Waldorf-Astoria Hotel, if it existed, had reputedly been used by President Franklin D. Roosevelt whenever he did not want his arrival in New York to be witnessed. Secret passages always exert a fascination, and this was my first real taste of Grand Central's mother lode of mysterious connections.

Late one night, escorted by my friends Hackett and Steve, I took a walk below Park Avenue, looking for track 61, which we had read was adjacent to the hotel connection. Since there were no public tracks numbered in the 60s, we simply walked off the platforms across the rails in the direction of the hotel. We had not gone far when a worker on a catwalk spotted us and asked us what the hell we were doing walking on live tracks. Rather sheepishly we told him that we were looking for a rumored secret exit from the station. To our surprise, he was sympathetic to our interest in the tunnels.

Leading us into a maintenance area to the right of the tracks, he told us that he had worked at the station for 20 years and was still mystified by it himself. He had heard of abandoned passages along here, but thought they had all been sealed off. On the other hand, he could point to an area in the tunnels where an Irish girl had hanged herself and where a co-worker of his had gotten sucked in and killed by a moving train. After chatting for a while, we ventured a question about something far more important than

*Figure 13.2 The entrance to one of the terminal's loops*

any hotel connection, namely, the greatest mystery of the New York underground of all time: how many levels deep is Grand Central?

This apparently simple question has been a continuous subject of debate. There are only two track levels—which themselves run at various depths—but how far down do the maintenance areas stretch? In the station's descriptions in their books on subterranean New York, the authors Pamela Jones and Jennifer Toth mention seven levels. A former terminal employee claims there are only six—two for the trains and four for utilities. The authors of *Grand Central: Gateway to a Million Lives*, however, speak of a power supply room eight stories down, and the formerly homeless Tina S., who lived in these catacombs for four years, speaks of a labyrinth of eerie caves and crawlspaces far beneath the lowest track level.

"How many underground levels are there?" we now asked our new friend. "Fifteen," he said. We were speechless. "There is one small staircase that goes down 15 levels. But I never went all the way to the bottom." He had descended several stories and encountered many things down there, from giant rats to drug addicts. "But I would never go down 15 stories. Who knows what the hell is down there?"

Yes, who knows? And why does this continue to be so intriguing? The sheer scope of the excavations makes it highly improbable that there is even one staircase going beyond the power station—which lies on bedrock 105 feet beneath the concourse. But the remarkable fact remains that even people who come in continuous intimate contact with this terminal resort to devising their own theories as to its layout. And yet the number of levels is only one of the many mysteries that lingered in the course of this station's turbulent construction history.

Grand Central Terminal evolved out of a depot that had been built along 42nd Street by the New York and Harlem Railroad, whose horse carriages and later steam trains provided service from Prince Street to Harlem as of the 1830s. Initially the line stopped at the foot of what is now Carnegie Hill near 96th Street, until a tunnel was blasted through the hill and the tracks were extended north. Further south, from 34th to 39th streets, the line had to tackle another obstacle, Murray Hill, by going through an open cut. After this segment was roofed over in 1850, the tunnel was used by horse cars and trolleys. It also had a station inside, a few remnants of which were left when it was modified into today's car tunnel.

*Figure 13.3 Cornelius Vanderbilt opened the original Grand Central Depot in 1871*

Grand Central, as such, was created by Commodore Cornelius Vanderbilt, a shipping magnate who had made savvy investments in several rail companies, including the Harlem Railroad, and became the president of New York Central in 1867. The Harlem Railroad owned the property between 42nd and 48th streets and Lexington and Madison avenues. Vanderbilt had great ambitions for his railroad business and decided that Manhattan needed a new, impressive passenger station, for which that parcel of land was perfect.

The commodore's plans were met with great amusement by New York society. Who would ever travel all the way up to 42nd Street, an area bounded by slaughterhouses and slums, to get on a train? But Vanderbilt pursued his vision and opened Grand Central Depot in 1871, stunning even his critics. The ornate building, the country's largest train station, had facilities stretching across 20 city blocks and was dazzling in size alone. It soon became a popular tourist attraction.

After the commodore's death, Grand Central stayed in the hands of the Vanderbilt family, and while its importance as a transit hub continued to grow, the depot building's days were numbered. By the end of the nineteenth century the amount of steam trains, with their by-products of noise and soot, was leading to complaints by residents north of the station. But the real impetus behind a new law in 1903, which banned steam locomotives from entering Manhattan after 1908, was a severe accident. Inside the Carnegie Hill tunnel, a train from White Plains

*Figure 13.4 Grand Central's original railyard in 1905, before it was moved underground*

*Figure 13.5 The new terminal building opened in 1913*

smashed into another train waiting on the tracks, killing 15 passengers. The tunnel had been filled with so much smoke that the train operator couldn't see the signals. There was a great public outcry, and the railroad found itself forced to switch to an electrified system within five years if it wanted to stay in business.

The engineer William Wilgus stepped up to the formidable task. Not only did the entire system need to be converted to electrification, but additional space had to be created for the third rails. Wilgus had a brilliant solution—instead of reconstructing the station on a horizontal level, it would expand vertically. In the future, trains were going to enter the terminal on two levels, the local trains on the lower level and the long-distance trains above them. To prevent the ceilings from collapsing under the immense weight of the station areas, they would be built as a series of underground bridges. Additionally, Wilgus planned separate platforms for arriving and departing trains, which would be connected by a loop on each level.

Above the underground station would rise a tremendous complex of hotels, banks, and offices, and this "Terminal City" was going to finance the reconstruction. Not only would many of these buildings have direct connections to the station, but there would be a separate track area beneath the post office on Lexington Avenue to facilitate mail delivery from the trains. The design of the terminal building was the creation of the architect Whitney Warren, who had studied at the École des

Beaux-Arts in Paris. His vision was an edifice that would distract passengers from the mundane hassles of commuting by evoking the romanticism of world travel.

The construction of the new track areas, which lasted from 1903 until 1912, was a logistical nightmare. More than three million cubic yards of rock and soil had to be excavated to move the train yard underground, with regular train service running all the while. Tracks were taken out of service one by one, while the blasting proceeded 45 feet below the street. Additional trains were required to dump the excavated soil into the Hudson River.

The fact that Pennsylvania Station opened during this time amidst great fanfare was annoying. But the inauguration of Grand Central Terminal in February 1913 was met with enormous applause, and the contemporary press, never modest about flaunting New York's engineering wonders, proclaimed the new structure to be the greatest station in the world.

Terminal City and the train yards were not finished until the 1930s. In 1929, the power plant on Park Avenue made way for the new Waldorf-Astoria Hotel. Like the other three adjacent hotels—the Ambassador, the Biltmore, and the Commodore—the Waldorf was accessible from the underground station area.

*Figure 13.6  Today, Grand Central is wedged between high-rises*

Grand Central Terminal nearly fell victim to the success of Vanderbilt's original gamble. Starting in the 1950s, as the property values around Terminal City kept soaring, there were many proposals to demolish the station or top it with an office tower. By then the amount of passengers was steadily declining, and, as a great blow to Grand Central, Amtrak was taking over New York's entire long-distance train service in 1971—with an exclusive connection to Penn Station. The fact that the structure survived intact is largely due to the efforts of Jacqueline Kennedy Onassis and the Municipal Art Society. In 1978 the Supreme Court preserved Grand Central's landmark status and prevented the erection of an office building on its roof.

In 1986 the deteriorating building underwent a major renovation, and since then the station's interior has become increasingly upscale. A former private office, which subsequently served as a wine cellar until becoming a facility for the MTA police in the 1980s, has been turned into the Campbell Apartment, an ostentatious bar. Most elegant is the subterranean Oyster Bar, with vaulted ceilings by the Italian architect Rafael Guastavino, who also designed the tiled vaults of

*Figure 13.7  The outer loop track of the lower track level*

the original City Hall station. The tiles outside the Oyster Bar's entrance have been arranged so that even very low sounds can travel from one corner to another, giving this area the name of the "Whispering Gallery."

Beyond the polished concourse, the most interesting parts of the structure unfold. There are numerous utility and maintenance areas on the two levels beneath the lower tracks, including a baggage tunnel below 45th Street. Beneath 46th Street is a six-foot-wide sewer and below 43rd and 49th streets are large water tanks that can be utilized in case of fire or a main break.

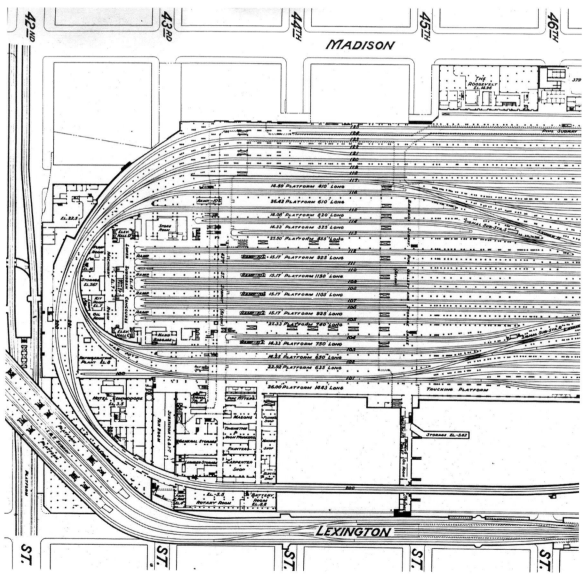

*Figure 13.8  Blueprint of lower level tracks*

Quite a bit deeper, 105 feet beneath the street, is the dynamo room, where five massive rotary converters once supplied power to the station. In 1929, when the original power plant at Park Avenue and 49th Street had to make way for the new Waldorf-Astoria Hotel, a giant vault was excavated below the Graybar Building at 43rd Street. This new substation, built inside the 250-foot-long cavern, was connected to the hotel site by a series of tunnels—and the old power operations were moved to their new home entirely underground. During World War II, soldiers were stationed here, guarding the top secret entrances from any possible sabotage that could have impacted the deployment of troops.

Even with these precautions, the power operations could not be entirely protected. Sheldon Lustig, who worked in the bowels of Grand Central in the 1970s, remembers when the whole terminal was shut down during the second blackout of that decade. Not only were the trains unable to run, but the pumps stopped working, and since most of the generating plant lies below sea level, it was soon flooded. After the water was finally pumped out, the dynamos had to be dried by covering them with plastic sheets and using hot air fans before they could be put back in service. By now they have become obsolete.

Also beneath the track levels, and extending over large parts of the station, is a labyrinth of steam pipes with a combined length of more than 60 miles. The main pipe gallery has been called "Burma Road" because of its moist heat, which has made it into a popular refuge for the homeless.[1]

In the early 1990s, when the amount of homeless residents at Grand Central likely reached its peak, up to 700 people sought shelter near the steam ducts, abandoned tracks, or other inconspicuous station areas every night. The renovation made it much more difficult for the homeless people to sleep here, however, because it has become harder to access the terminal's areas inconspicuously. Tina S., who has written a book about living in the station's hidden areas for four years, mentioned in an interview in 2001 how difficult it was to get to her former crawlspaces. "You can't really climb below the tracks like we used to," she said. "I don't know where all the homeless people disappeared to."

To tunnel explorers, the riches of Burma Road may be the most irresistible part of the station, but subway buffs have other areas to whet their appetites. The subway, which does not enter the two track levels, is connected to the commuter rails by a series of passages and shares subterranean space with the terminal in

---

[1.] Burma Road has also been mentioned in another context. In 1987 a group of 130 workers sued the Metro North Commuter Railroad—the MTA branch responsible for commuter service—for medical benefits. These electricians, welders, and pipe layers were called the "Snowmen of Grand Central" because they would emerge from their work among the steampipes covered in white dust, which turned out to be asbestos. However, the Supreme Court ruled against the employees, since the one worker used in the test case had not shown signs of illness.

*Figure 13.9  A rest area for weary souls at the end of a disused track*

more ways than meets the eye. A pipe gallery placed by the IRT in 1909, which inadvertently cut through underground spaces planned for use by commuter trains, is just one example of this.

One question in the subway area revolves around August Belmont's private car, the Mineola. Near the basement bar of his hotel, there had to be a door that led directly to the tracks, from where he used to mount his "Minnie." While the Belmont Hotel no longer exists, the original south bound IRT track is still there, used by trains accessing the shuttle to Times Square. The original north bound track in this area, according to the graffiti writer Smith, is buried under debris. Somewhere in this vicinity, the Mineola must have stood waiting on the tracks.

The remnant of the Steinway tunnel loop is another interesting indicator of subway history here. This tunnel (also known as the Belmont Tunnel) was initially used by trolleys running beneath the East River from Queens to the Grand Central area, where they would turn around in a loop. The trolleys were soon taken out of service to be replaced by the 7 line of the subway. When the subway station for Grand Central was built, the old loop had to be perforated in two areas, one for each

*laid-up train below City Hall faces a flooded track bed covered with World Trade Center d*

*A track of the BMT City Hall station's unfinished lower level*

*Flooded track beds wind from City Hall toward the Woolworth Building*

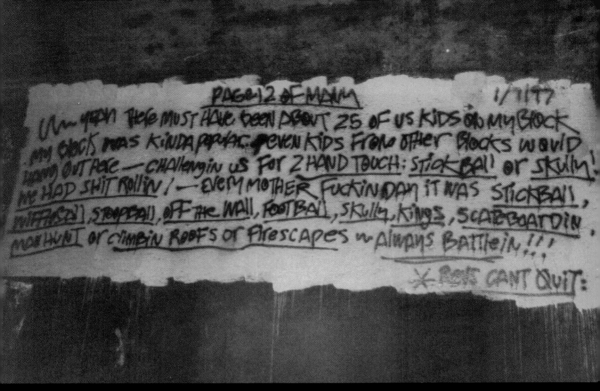

PAGE 12 OF MAM                                    1/7/97

Um yeah there must have been about 25 of us kids on my block
my block was kinda popular, even kids from other blocks would
hang out here — challengin us for 2 hand touch, stickball or skully!
we had shit rollin / — every mother fuckin day it was STICKBALL,
muffball, stoopball, off the wall, football, skully, kings, scateboardin
manhunt or climbin roofs or firescapes n always battlein!!!
                                        ✗ REVS CANT QUIT:

*One of Revs's 235 autobiographical pages in the subway system*

*An unused subway tunnel below Central Park*

*Groundwater has seeped into a section of this tunnel below 63rd Street*

*The classic concourse of Grand Central*

*The lower level loop of Grand Central Terminal*

*Grand Central's tracks converge before leading north below Park Avenue*

*One of the many emergency exits in the heart of Grand Central Terminal*

*Figure 13.10 An interpretation of track levels below 42nd Street,
showing a planned Jersey connection*

track, so the trains could continue to Times Square. The loop was therefore cut into three sections, which reportedly provided another refuge for the homeless at one time, making this another intriguing area for further investigations. Traces of the bellmouths can still be seen from the 7 train outside the Grand Central station.

Also apparently abandoned and sealed off were the first steps toward a connection between Grand Central Terminal and McAdoo's Hudson tubes to New Jersey. That this stretch exists at all has been vehemently denied by some rail authorities who argue that McAdoo's tunnels belonged to the PRR, New York Central's competitor, thus ruling out such a collaboration. But negotiations for a Jersey connection are on record and some early diagrams indicate a tunnel area for the McAdoo line parallel to 42nd Street, and more than one Grand Central worker has claimed that the construction on this was actually begun.

But Grand Central has even more to quicken the heartbeat of the underground explorer—three ghost stations in the main tunnel under Park Avenue. The platforms

*Figure 13.11 The abandoned inner loop track was fenced off from the public station area in 2002*

at 59th and 72nd streets belonged to stations that were never finished, although their staircases to Park Avenue are still intact. The station at 86th Street, however, was used until 1903, before the excavations for the new terminal began. All three stations now serve as emergency exits and can be clearly seen from passing trains.

By now it was 2:00 A.M. and the station had been closed for a half hour. The worker who had addressed us as we wandered across the tracks, and who declined to show us the stairs descending 15 levels, escorted us to one of the numerous private exits through which we could inconspicuously return to the street. We thanked him and began to ascend a dark staircase next to what looked like a freight elevator, when he called to us. "By the way," he said, "this used to be the private entrance used by Franklin D. Roosevelt." Surprisingly, when we opened the door at the end of the hallway ahead, we found ourselves stepping out of a side door in the Waldorf-Astoria Hotel onto the street.

The former Biltmore Hotel also had a direct connection. A tunnel next to the Vanderbilt's office in the hotel led beneath Vanderbilt Avenue near a station area

*Figure 13.12  Sealed passages and stairways abound at Grand Central*

*Figure 13.13  Former loop tracks on the lower level*

that in more recent times was occupied by Off-Track Betting. Joe Schipani, a former employee of the Biltmore Hotel, reports, "If we couldn't find one of our workers, the first thing we would do would be to go through the tunnel to OTB, and more than likely we would find our man."

The possible remnants of another hotel entrance, to the former Commodore (now the Grand Hyatt), may lie in a maintenance section of the terminal's lower loop. The outer and inner loop tracks are separated by a wall with niches resembling those in the subway system, which, in the dim yellow lights, evoke a catacomb-like atmosphere. They embrace the terminal's core one level beneath the lower concourse, an area mainly occupied by maintenance rooms. The inner tracks are not only rusted and broken, but are partially buried beneath a work shed. Before the terror attacks in 2001 and the construction of a fence that disables such excursions, I used to enjoy wandering around this area, since it led to several fascinating locations.

The doors leading into the maintenance areas are open, and there is always much activity: steam wafts out, machines clatter, and above a deserted landing there is a constant dripping from the ceiling. In this area the frequently occurring, old-style sign "Look out for trains" has been altered to read "Look out for rain."

*Figure 13.14  There are two kinds of rats at Grand Central: giant and supergiant*

Further back, in an open space where the largest rat I have ever seen darted across my path, the same sign has been changed to "Look out for rats." It's good to know they stay on top of things down here.

The sounds of machines and workers fade into an electrified hum once the loop is navigated and one continues north into the general track area. The only graffiti here are the markings left by workers in orange paint. The edges of the entire underground area are lined with emergency exits and occasional stairs between the two track levels. One of these staircases initially reminded me of being in a ruin inside a forest. The steps were covered with layers of debris resembling mulch, and it seemed that no one had come here in years. There are other unexpected discoveries, such as a sewer manhole cover from 1874, only three years after Vanderbilt opened the original depot.

Back near the loop, in the area where my old blueprint of Grand Central's underground levels indicates a staircase to the Commodore Hotel, I came across a cinderblocked door. Could this have been the entrance to the hotel? According to my maps, the connecting passage lay between the refrigeration plant and a

*Figure 13.15 Remnant of the old depot: a sewer cover from 1874*

storage room, and that is where this door is located. The small room near the sealed entrance is empty but for an old Christmas wreath, which looks as if it has weathered many holidays down here.

## ANOTHER TRACK LEVEL ON THE HORIZON

One major change at Grand Central Terminal is currently in preparation—a long-awaited connection to the Long Island Rail Road. This is the largest construction project yet attempted by the MTA. Currently the only way to access the LIRR in Manhattan is at Penn Station, which makes any transfer to the Metro-North trains at Grand Central very inconvenient. This connection, which has been in discussion since the 1970s, is expected to be completed in 2011.

Because the third rails at Grand Central are incompatible with those used by the LIRR, an entirely new terminal will be built: beyond and beneath the two existing levels, another track level will be created. The trains will enter Manhattan through the 63rd Street tunnel, which runs under the East River parallel to the Queensboro Bridge. From there the track will turn and run beneath Park Avenue, dipping below the subway tunnels of the N and R lines.

The MTA expects to excavate nearly a billion cubic yards of soil, which will be removed through the 63rd Street tunnel into Long Island City. In the 1970s, this tunnel was planned with two levels—the upper for subway service and the lower for the LIRR. Trenches were dug in the East River, into which the four completed tunnel sections were sunk, which were then connected with a tube through Roosevelt Island. The original plan had included a new LIRR terminal at 48th Street and Third Avenue, yet this was scrapped during the construction for financial reasons. Even before the project was completed, officials knew that the lower level for the LIRR tracks would not be used. Nonetheless, they had to finish the tunnel as planned or risk structural damage. The project, which was completed at the same time as one of the segments of the Second Avenue subway, became an embarrassment to the MTA.

In 1980 the lower level of the tunnel was officially abandoned and its connecting staircases to the subway above were sealed. The empty passage became a favorite site for graffiti writers, until cameras were installed there in recent years to prevent potential terrorist attacks on the subaquatic tube. Once the excavations get under way, those cameras may inadvertently record one of the largest soil removal projects in the history of the city.

part IV  Historic Rail Tunnels

*Figure 14.1  A freight tunnel of the LIRR's Bay Ridge line*

# CHAPTER FOURTEEN

# An Overview

New York has a host of tunnels that were abandoned after either partial completion or being used only briefly. This includes traces of unfinished highways, such as the beginnings of the Lower Manhattan Expressway, constructed underground at Chrystie and Broome streets in 1962. Yet no matter how deeply they are buried, car tunnels are just not very captivating. While the Brooklyn-Battery Tunnel, for instance, may be the country's longest underwater car tunnel, and has a noteworthy, highly guarded vent structure directly next to Governors Island, traversing it is more of a nuisance than an underground adventure. Rail tunnels and abandoned right-of-ways, on the other hand, often filled with burned-out cars, furniture, stray dogs, and laid-up freight trains — visited only by rail buffs, graffiti writers, and the homeless — are perfect for adventurous and romantic walks.

The Bay Ridge Branch of the LIRR, which once served passengers but is now only used by freight trains, has two interesting underground areas. One is an unusual subterranean space near the waterfront in Bay Ridge, which is referred to by local graffiti writers as King Kong's Cave, where the tracks pass beneath two tall apartment buildings supported on stilts inside an open cut in the rock, creating a strange cavernous terrain. Further toward Long Island, the line passes through the East New York Tunnel, a half-mile-long underground stretch containing an abandoned station that last saw passenger service in 1924. The passage accommodates four tracks, each in its own tunnel and with its own portals, and the train laid up next to the abandoned platform seems to be a permanent fixture by now. Aside from providing refuge for the homeless, both of these areas are very desolate.

If it is actually completed, a major freight tunnel, currently in the planning stage, should have a large impact on the surrounding neighborhoods. The proposed Cross Harbor Freight Tunnel is intended to provide a link from New

Figure 14.2  The East New York Tunnel with its abandoned station on the right

Figure 14.3  Vent structure for the Brooklyn-Battery Tunnel next to Governors Island

Jersey to Bay Ridge, and continue from there to Maspeth in Queens. New York depends heavily on truck deliveries across the various bridges, and this rail tunnel would not only alleviate the daily freight transport, but would also come in handy in case of further terror attacks, which is why the project has just received the Port Authority's approval. But the tunnel may not be built for another decade — about the same time a new Hudson River tunnel might be constructed to relieve congestion at Penn Station.

Of all the rail tunnels in New York, there are two that are particularly remarkable, and these, the Atlantic Avenue Tunnel and the Freedom Tunnel, are looked at more closely in the chapters that follow.

*Figure 15.1 Atlantic Avenue in the early nineteenth century*

# CHAPTER FIFTEEN

# The Lost Tunnel of Atlantic Avenue

In the summer of 1911, the Brooklyn newspaper, the *Brooklyn Daily Eagle*, challenged a group of 75 men to find the location of a mysterious abandoned tunnel — the first subway tunnel in America.

Apparently it had been constructed below Atlantic Avenue as part of a rail line from Brooklyn to Long Island, and when the route was discontinued in 1861, it was closed. Why this had happened, and whether any remnants of the thoroughfare still existed, had long been subject to speculation, and the rumors persisted even after the *Eagle's* fruitless investigation.

Almost half a century later, Robert Daley resuscitated the myths surrounding the lost passage in his 1959 book *The World Beneath the City*. One of the chapters, entitled "The Curious and the Bizarre," was pessimistic about the chances of the subterranean structure ever being found again: "And so the tunnel stays empty and dark, occupied only by its legends . . . Nor is anyone likely to enter it during the next hundred years. Unless perhaps it's a smuggler, a murderer or a saboteur."

It was an engineering student who, 20 years later, decided to get to the bottom of the mystery once and for all. Even before he had heard of the rumors, the native Brooklynite Bob Diamond suspected that something monumental lay virtually beneath his feet. One night, when he was 12 years old and trying to sleep — so his story goes — he was suddenly aware of the strong smell of a steam locomotive, which seemed to come through his open bedroom window. At the same time, he had a vision of an old masonry tunnel with a magnificently constructed brick arch. The next day he asked around the neighborhood whether anyone knew of such a structure in the area. He was told about the rumors, but no one could tell him anything more specific.

He was attending the Pratt Institute as an engineering student in 1979 when he next heard about the abandoned passage. Someone on a local radio station mentioned that a few people had claimed to hear ghostly train sounds beneath a

*Figure 15.2  The Atlantic Avenue Tunnel*

street in Brooklyn. According to the announcer, local residents had been speculating about old steam trains in Brooklyn's underground for decades, but no one had ever found a trace of the tunnel that supposedly still lay buried there. Diamond decided to investigate the rumors. He examined every blueprint of Brooklyn he could get his hands on, until he finally came across a document indicating the exact location of a tunnel below Atlantic Avenue.

The Long Island Rail Road had connected Brooklyn with the rest of the island as early as 1832. At the time, a ferry service from Manhattan brought passengers to a rail station in Brooklyn Heights, where Atlantic Avenue hit the shore of the East River. The area was well populated even then, supporting about 40,000 residents, and competition with Manhattan along the waterfront was thriving. But the railroad's initial stretch from this Brooklyn terminal was problematic. The route led uphill, which meant that the trains of this early model required horses to tackle the incline. On the other side of the hill, the route led toward the center of Long Island and continued into Boston, relying on ferries for part of the way.

In 1844, the LIRR obtained permission to build a tunnel through Cobble Hill, which would allow the steam locomotives to proceed on an even grade without the assistance of horses. This harmonized beautifully with the schemes of city officials, who were hoping to turn Atlantic Avenue into one of the most scenic, commercially desirable boulevards on the East Coast. The street was going to be lined with trees and sophisticated establishments to attract the Brooklyn gentry. The loud and noxious locomotives were no longer welcome to share the road with carriages and pedestrians.

It took less than a year to build a tunnel wide enough for two tracks, reaching from Columbia Place to Boerum Place. An open cut was constructed in the street and then covered with a wide masonry arch. The tunnel was nearly 2,000 feet long, 21 feet wide, and 17 feet high at the top of the arch.

During the inaugural ride in December 1844, the train stopped halfway inside the tunnel so the attending dignitaries could get out and admire the masonry construction. But the tunnel was so full of smoke from the two locomotives — in the front and rear of the train — that only a few passengers ventured out, mainly to assure themselves that there really were tunnel walls behind the black plumes.

*Figure 15.3 Rail service along this stretch was discontinued in 1859*

Nonetheless, it seemed that everyone in the area soon flocked to Atlantic Avenue to admire the exquisite construction and experience the unusual subterranean journey. The poet Walt Whitman later captured the atmosphere of this train ride:

> The old tunnel, that used to lie there under ground, a passage of Acheron-like solemnity and darkness, now all closed and filled up, and soon to be utterly forgotten. . . . The tunnel dark as the grave, cold, damp, and silent. How beautiful [to] look at earth and heaven again, as . . . we emerge from the gloom!

But this new thoroughfare did not quite succeed in making Atlantic Avenue more beautiful. The steam from the locomotives was vented into the street through several tall smokestacks in the tunnel's ceiling. Not only the street itself, but especially the elegant houses along the avenue, began to accumulate a coat of soot, and the local residents and shop owners did not wait long to complain about the pollution. Even as the frequency of the trains lessened over the years, the protests continued.

When a court ruled in favor of the residents in 1859 by passing the Atlantic Avenue Tunnel Act to bar all steam locomotives from the area, the LIRR was forced to remove its trains from this stretch. The original tracks were dismantled, and in 1861 the tunnel was sealed. For a short time afterward, it was rented out as storage space to various private enterprises, while some members of the community still hoped that it would be reopened some day.

In the meantime, Atlantic Avenue was still waiting for the beautification that would turn it into a Brooklyn version of the Champs Élysées in Paris. But now, without the rail connection to Manhattan, manufacturers and shop owners turned their backs on the neighborhood. The area quickly deteriorated. The elegant hotels began shutting their doors, many shops were forced to relocate, while saloons and seedier establishments moved in.

The mystique of the abandoned tunnel, however, remained. Since it had played a large role in the economic rise and fall of the area, it was no wonder the tunnel began to stimulate the imagination of the locals. Fanciful stories began to arise about what the dark, empty space might have harbored since its closure. One of the most popular early legends concerned smugglers using the tunnel as a hiding place shortly after the Civil War. A few cleverly concealed entrance points had reputedly been left uncovered, and one of these lay close enough to the water's edge for the smugglers to anchor their boats and slip inside without attracting much attention from the police.

An article in the *Brooklyn Daily Eagle* in 1896 addressed the tales that were circulating about the lost thoroughfare, whose exact topographic features were by now quickly fading from public memory. If the tunnel did really still exist, the

*Figure 15.4  A trench connects the manhole entrance with the tunnel portal*

reporter wrote, only one thing was certain: it would be an ideal space to grow mushrooms in. But the writer searched in vain for an entrance, or for anyone who had set foot inside it since it had been sealed.

Yet over the decades, the tunnel was searched for and entered, only to pass again into oblivion. In 1936, after receiving a letter that gangsters were disposing dead bodies inside, the police undertook a fruitless search for the lost thoroughfare, combing through the cellars of various establishments along Atlantic Avenue. Although they eventually had to tear up the street to get inside, they found nothing remarkable in the tunnel. Their investigation showed that it had also been accessed in 1916 by employees of the Bureau of Highways and Sewers. At that time, the worker crew had entered it with the aid of electric hand lamps, to investigate whether any recent utility work had structurally damaged the masonry arch.

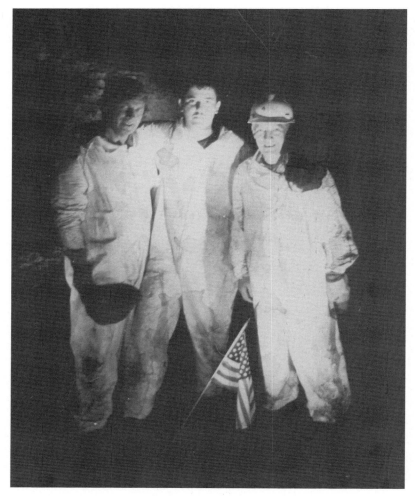

*Figure 15.5  Diamond's photo of his fellow adventurers after the tunnel discovery*

The blueprint that Diamond found in 1980 showed a manhole entrance at the intersection of Atlantic Avenue and Court Street. After the first manhole he opened led only to a layer of dirt, he asked for the assistance of Brooklyn Union Gas, which owned another manhole nearby. The utility was willing to give him access, but not before outfitting him with a gas mask, an oxygen tank, and a two-way radio. The foreman gave him only five minutes, then the workers would pull Diamond up by the rope they had fastened around his chest.

Diamond dropped onto the layer of dirt beneath the opening and crawled along the narrow space that stretched ahead beneath the asphalt. He spotted tall heaps of soil in the distance. And behind those, a brick wall — the sealed end of the tunnel. When he reached the portal, he rapidly dug through the dirt with his hands, hoping for an entrance. Sure enough, after a few minutes he uncovered the top edge of a sealed doorway.

Breathlessly, he let the workers know about his discovery and asked them to join him, preferably equipped with "Sicilian toothpicks" — six-foot-long crowbars. Several men climbed down, although there was barely enough room for everyone in the narrow space. They beat against the wall until they finally broke through.

"It was as if we were suddenly in outer space," Diamond says. From the depths of the black hole a cold breeze swept against their faces. When they shone their flashlights into the tunnel, it appeared infinitely long. The pebbles in the ceiling sparkled like stars.

The bottom of the passage lay about 12 feet beneath the opening, too far for them to jump down. Diamond resurfaced and bought a rope ladder at a nearby hardware store. The men were awestruck when they descended into the tunnel. It was completely preserved, a world all its own. Old shoes and bottles emerged into the rays of their flashlights as they gingerly stepped through the darkness. It was utterly silent — they might just as well have been in a tomb at the end of the earth. They had no idea how far the tunnel would lead. "I think we're in New Jersey," one of the workers said after they had finally traversed the entire length.

After Diamond made his discovery public, not only city and government officials, but many historians and scientists, climbed down the manhole to examine

*Figure 15.6 The west end of the tunnel was sealed off and backfilled*

the tunnel's properties, take soil samples, and analyze the artifacts strewn across the track beds. Diamond obtained the city's permission to make the tunnel accessible to the public and began clearing out a safe entryway, subsequently replacing the rope ladder with a staircase and installing electric lights.

He discovered three openings in the ceiling, the remnants of the ventilation shafts used to divert steam onto the street. After the tunnel's closure, the chimneys had simply been smashed down into the openings and now lay in broken heaps on the ground. He also found shards and other relics that hinted at one of the tunnel's rumored functions — the manufacture of gin during Prohibition. Rumor had it that the booze was funneled directly into a tap disguised as a water pipe in a saloon on Atlantic Avenue.

Another discovery was an inscription on the wall from March 11, 1916, which stated that "Lynch put first electric light into the subway." To his visitors inquiring about the graffiti, Diamond likes to tell the story that the tunnel was a suspected hideout for Germans manufacturing mustard gas during the First World War. He claims that after an explosion inside the "Black Tom" munitions factory across the New York Bay in New Jersey, two FBI agents decided to investigate the lost thoroughfare they had heard of, managed to break a hole into the tunnel's ceiling, and memorialized their experience on the wall. It does make for a much more dramatic story than tracing the graffiti back to those sewer workers who entered with electric lamps in 1916.

After founding the Brooklyn Historic Railway Association, Diamond received permission to lease the tunnel from the city as an exhibition space, although he only rarely opens it for public tours. The original manhole remains the only entry point. Visitors can climb down a small ladder and walk along a narrow corridor hewn through backfill, until they reach the original opening in the wall above the staircase. On one occasion in the spring of 2002, the tunnel was also host to its only formal evening event, when Dark Passage organized a banquet and sound installation there. The theme of the evening was World War I espionage — an homage to the purported FBI graffiti.

One mystery surrounding the tunnel remains unsolved. Diamond has not been able to access the entire tunnel. During its closure, the final segment leading to the river shore was blocked off by another masonry wall. According to his research, one of the locomotives had derailed near the terminal, and rather than repair and remove it, the rail company took out only the tracks before sealing the space. He believes that the locomotive is still buried there today.

A local resident, who used to play in the basement of 64 Atlantic Avenue as a child, remembers digging a hole through a damaged part of the basement floor and

*Figure 15.7  Graffiti left by sewer inspectors in 1916*

discovering an open space beyond, where he reportedly spotted an old locomotive. His description, including the detail that the wheels were larger than those of the trains he knew from western movies, coincided with contemporary reports of the locomotive's design.

Unfortunately, the house has since been demolished; its foundation lies obstructed by the supports of the Brooklyn Queens Expressway. Since the backfill behind the rear wall of the tunnel was too difficult to remove, Diamond applied for and received permission to dig three holes near the intersection of Atlantic Avenue and Hicks Street in 1990. He and his team did reach another segment of the original passage, and photos of a small entrance hole provide a glimpse of an ornamental wall next to a cavernous subterranean space.

Before he was able to continue the excavation, however, the city retracted its permission and resurfaced the street. Since then, no further efforts to open the rest of the tunnel have been made. Although the locomotive is likely only a part of Brooklyn lore, the remaining hidden passage would still be exciting to uncover. Perhaps this mystery will be left for another explorer to solve.

*Figure 16.1  Large vents illuminate the Freedom Tunnel*

CHAPTER SIXTEEN

# The Freedom Tunnel

IN GREEK MYTHOLOGY, THE DOG WHO GUARDS THE ENTRANCE to the underworld was given the name Cerberus. Whether the dog at the entrance to the Freedom Tunnel also had a name is questionable. He stands next to the tracks where the tunnel begins to dip beneath Riverside Park, although to describe him as standing may be a bit of an exaggeration. Propped up between an old shoe and a stick, one of his two sides covered with spray paint, the flattened carcass can barely still be recognized as a dog.

Whether a visitor to the tunnel laughs at this or takes it as a creepy sign of worse things ahead might depend on the time of day. In the morning, the Freedom Tunnel is a spectacular sight. The sunlight entering through the large air vents in the ceiling forms a continuous pattern, showing the tunnel's tremendous scope and illuminating the many murals throughout.

At night, however, this territory is particularly sketchy, not so much because of the trains, which barrel to and from Penn Station at long intervals, but because the tunnel is still populated with occasional residents and other visitors. The community of people who had made their homes here, documented most extensively in Marc Singer's film *Dark Days* and Margaret Morton's photo book *The Tunnel*, no longer exists to such an organized degree. When the train service was temporarily discontinued through this tunnel in 1980, the homeless settled in abandoned maintenance shacks, constructed rooms out of plywood, and refurbished the large stairwells. The estimates of the amount of people living down here until 1995 range from fifty to several hundred.

In 1995, however, the fire department ordered the destruction of the makeshift homes. For the next two years, the worker houses and shacks were torn down, and the homeless dispersed. Whereas one of the residents named Bernard, the self-proclaimed "Lord of the Tunnel," had maintained a degree of order and civility in the community, the area subsequently became more dangerous. A friend of mine

*Figure 16.2 Maintenance and storage areas inside the tunnel have been taken over by the homeless*

who frequents this place once found a corpse lying next to the tracks at night. Now he avoids this part of the underground after sunset.

The 2.5-mile-long tunnel belongs to what was once the lifeline of New York. In 1850, when the Hudson River Railroad planned a freight connection between Manhattan and Albany, tracks were laid directly next to the Hudson. Along this route, produce and dairy items were delivered from farms in the north, and poultry and other meat products were brought directly to the Stock Yards Company Building on 41st Street. As a result of this line, many more factories sprang up in the meatpacking district and other areas on the west side.

The trains ran right next to the streets until 1934, when the West Side Improvement Project was initiated to clear the streets for vehicular traffic. As part of the project, the tracks were to disappear in an open cut north of 35th Street. To

*Figure 16.3 Left behind*

the south, the line was to rise into a viaduct by means of a loop, without ever crossing a street. When the project was finished, the tracks led from the Bronx to a terminal on Spring Street, with railyards at 30th and 60th streets, where trains could be stored and the freight was redistributed. To facilitate delivery, the viaduct led directly through several buildings in the meatpacking district. The casualties of these developments were 640 demolished buildings and the West Side Cowboys. Previously, every train moving downtown along the Hudson had been preceded by a man on horseback, waving a red flag to warn traffic of the approaching train, which inched along behind him at a speed of six miles an hour.

The tracks between 72nd and 125th streets also saw a substantial change. Even back in the 1870s, Frederick Law Olmsted had designed plans for a park that ended at a road along the Hudson. As part of the West Side Improvement Project, Riverside Park was to be extended further toward the Hudson, by covering the tracks inside a tunnel whose roof could inconspicuously blend into the landscape. When it was finished, only the occasional ventilation grates and emergency exits indicated the presence of the tunnel from the park surface.

By the 1970s, New York's former lifeline had become obsolete. The viaduct in Chelsea, known today as the High Line, continues its picturesque deterioration

*Figure 16.4 These bedrock ledges sometimes serve as campsites for the homeless.*

while awaiting a possible reuse as a promenade, having been saved from demolition by the organization Friends of the High Line. North of Penn Station the line was reopened by Amtrak in 1991 for passenger service to Albany. By that time the tunnel had long been taken over not only by the homeless but by graffiti writers, who have since continued to cover all available surfaces.

After a writer by the name of Freedom discovered the tunnel in the 1970s, he began painting his versions of such classics as the Mona Lisa and Dali's dripping clock on its walls. Together with Smith, Freedom painted an extraordinary series of murals, including a huge version of Goya's *Third of May*. It was Smith who first began calling the tunnel after Freedom.

Smith, who should have his own tunnel named after him, has wandered the entire west side freight line in one shot. Unlike most other visitors to that tunnel, he actually prefers walking in the dark by himself. On those occasions when he would encounter anyone down here, he would just say hello and continue. One area along the line, namely, a track spur that curves toward the waterfront, has changed significantly since his first visit there. This track—another spot frequented by the

*Figure 16.5 The end of the line near the Hudson*

homeless—leads between cliffs of blasted bedrock and stops dead at a large cavern bordering on the Hudson. Smith remembers coming here in 1984 with his late brother Sane, when this tunnel led directly into the river. The first time they discovered the space, they began wading from the track into the Hudson. "After being in a foot of water deep we turned back," he recounts. Subsequently the tunnel was closed up, only to turn into a disordered homeless camp. Then, as now, people had also pitched shelters on top of the rocky ledges.

Today the Freedom Tunnel is almost a kind of museum of New York City's wilder past, with its profligate graffiti and traces of anarchic living, and hopefully it will remain as such. Like the rest of the city, it seems more subdued in recent years; those people who have moved back are more careful to hide their presence. This increased secrecy may come from wanting to avoid authorities, but may also stem from a desire to be left alone in general. An unsavory by-product of the tunnel's documentation has been the "mole people tourism" sensationalized by some media

*Figure 16.6 A Freedom mural commemorates the evacuation of the tunnel's residents in 1995*

outlets, for whom the homeless seem to have replaced the circus freaks of old. Well, nothing to see here, folks. Most of the remnants of the original residencies have been removed by now, and only some former belongings still lie in heaps along the tracks—suitcases, frying pans, photos, shoes.

What is striking about a walk along these tracks are the sounds entering the tunnel through the vent shafts above, especially the laughter of children playing in the park. The sounds echo through the large space, making it seem as if the voices are coming from stairwells or the dark areas just beyond the tunnel's curve. Standing beneath one of the large grates, it is possible to watch someone play ball directly above the tracks in this upscale neighborhood park. Such a visceral contrast between wealth and poverty, sunlit nature and sketchy darkness, is rare even in New York—and it can be assumed that most visitors to Riverside Park have no idea of the world just below their feet.

part V Underground Passageways

*Figure 17.1  The New York waterfront in the 1880s*

CHAPTER SEVENTEEN
# Playgrounds of the Underworld

One day in June 1910, a jeweler on the Lower East Side received a strange, hand-written note, stating that a tunnel had been dug directly in front of his store at Grand and Ludlow streets and that two men were lying dead inside. When the street was opened up to begin a search for the bodies, the entire neighborhood came out to watch. Sure enough, starting from the basement of 53 Ludlow Street, a crude tunnel had been dug toward Grand Street, where it had caved in.

Two shafts were sunk in the street according to directions in the jeweler's note to look for anyone trapped inside the claustrophobic passage. The second shaft came a bit too close, severing the feet of Isaac Finkelstein, who had died in a fetal position next to the spoon and screwdriver with which he had been digging the tunnel. Although no other body was found, the police speculated that Finkelstein and several accomplices had planned to burrow to the basement next to the jeweler's, from where they could break into his store and disappear again with the spoils. The case kept the Lower East Side fascinated for weeks.

Secret passages and sinister activities go hand in hand, as every imaginative child can verify, and New York has a solid tradition of makeshift tunnels dug for nefarious ends, mostly in an era when the underground was not as crowded as it is now. Some of these tunnels were extremely rudimentary, and one might admire the determination of the thieves, willing to squeeze through nightmarishly tight burrows that could collapse on them at any moment. The long tunnel that was dug in 1861 for the robbery of the New York Exchange Bank at 185 Greenwich Street was only 18 inches high at its tallest point.

There were also larger tunnels, only somewhat more sophisticated, which provided inconspicuous access to buildings with only the barest structural reinforcements. One of these was discovered by two boys in September 1924 at Cherry and Pike streets, when they explored the pit beneath a caved-in sidewalk and ran to the police with an account of having found two skeletons inside a tunnel. Donning overalls, two detectives crawled 50 feet into the passage before they had to turn around, because its sides were beginning to collapse from the curious crowd assembling above. Since the tunnel led beneath one of the oldest buildings in lower New York, the police surmised that it was not a contemporary bootleggers' tunnel but dated much further back.

That particular discovery might have been one of the many tunnels in the notorious Fourth Ward described by Herbert Asbury in *The Gangs of New York*. There were frequent accounts of underground passages built on Manhattan's waterfront in the nineteenth century, connecting to hotels and seedier establishments for smuggling and kidnapping purposes. At that time the waterfront, particularly South Street, was a hotbed of disreputable activities. This included the practice of shanghaiing young men onto ships, which meant that they were knocked unconscious and woke up dazed and aching on a deck at sea, forced to labor under terrible conditions with no means of escape. In the Fourth Ward there were a slew of infamous cellar establishments with names like the Rat Pit and the Hell Hole along with ramshackle hotels, such as the East River Hotel, in which one murder took place in 1891 that led authorities to wonder if Jack the Ripper had come to New York. Some of these buildings provided their own underground means of escape and, at least according to contemporary lore, an inconspicuous way to transport the dead.

The practice of shanghaiing, which had declined around the end of the nineteenth century, blossomed again during Prohibition in the 1920s, when the men were abducted to "Rum Row," the ships that moved just outside the sphere of the Coast Guard to engage in the profitable alcohol trade. Each kidnapped person reportedly brought a reward of $100, and for some time South Street again became dangerous territory.

How many secret tunnels really existed along the waterfront is hard to tell, and they would have mostly disappeared during the many construction projects of the last century. But New York had no shortage of underground playgrounds for more modern hoodlums, who could always move into an abandoned space. One such enviable find was a tunnel beneath the south reservoir gatehouse in Central Park, which was taken over by a group of "hobos" and turned into a gambling hall. The entrance to what they called the Park Club was a long staircase inside the gatehouse caretaker's home, then abandoned, which ended at a tunnel leading underneath the reservoir. The space was furnished with tables, chintz curtains, and red lanterns, and here the men met nightly to play cards. They were only discovered after a money dispute outside the gatehouse was overheard by a cop.

One area with infamous tunnels that still exist today — a part of which can even be visited publicly — is Chinatown. There is a small street in Chinatown, where it

The Atlantic Avenue Tunnel

*A portal connects the Atlantic Avenue Tunnel to a manhole on the street*

*"The Lost Head of Mata Hari," a Dark Passage event, culminates inside the Atlantic Avenue Tunnel*

*This track, long disused, once belonged to a New York Central freight line*

*An obsolete freight track below Hell's Kitchen*

*Standing guard at the north entrance of the Freedom Tunnel*

*Legendary murals by Freedom and Smith*

*Mural detail showing scale*

*A mural by Freedom in the Riverside tunnel*

*Goya's famous painting, here rendered by Freedom and Smith,*
*takes on new meaning in the tunnel below Riverside Park*

*Figure 17.2  The site of a former opera house with tunnel access on Doyers Street*

has been said that more people have been murdered than in any other place of that size in America. Doyers Street, which branches off the Bowery and hangs a sharp curve, has also been called the "bloody angle."

Since its establishment in the 1870s, Chinatown has been ruled by several gangs known as tongs — which oversee the trade in merchandise and labor — and its streets have witnessed periods of incessant warfare, especially before a truce was called in the 1930s. By the end of the nineteenth century, the tongs were not only entrenched in New York's Chinatown but in other Chinese enclaves across the country, fighting for control of the opium trade, prostitution, and gambling.

In the 1890s, when New York was dominated by the On Leong tong, the area had become a popular destination for adventurers from the city's more affluent quarters who wanted to go on slumming tours. They visited the gambling establishments, brothels, and opium dens in Chinatown's cellars. The opium dens weren't necessarily furnished with the exotic splendor one might imagine, but might consist of a row of bunks hanging from hooks against a bare masonry wall. Nonetheless, the area exerted a seedy and glamorous attraction to many gentlemen of New York's high society, and the tongs were ready to relieve them of their money.

Arriving on the scene at the turn of the century, intent on domination, was a legendary character called Mock Duck, who soon took over the Hip Sing tong. This new gang leader spooked his rivals with his reckless behavior. Clad in a shirt of iron mail, armed with two pistols and a hatchet, he was known to squat in the middle of the street and fire blindly in all directions, yet he himself was never felled. Under his leadership, his tong became the On Leong's greatest enemy and soon took over the majority of Pell and Doyers streets.

Doyers Street was particularly well suited for battles. Not only did the sharp curve allow for surprises, but its buildings were interconnected through subterranean passages. From the tunnels of a brewery that had previously occupied the area, there had grown a labyrinth of narrow corridors, which the Chinese quickly took over. Inconspicuous hatches on the streets, along with adjoining basement areas, provided entrances into the passages. This meant that the fighters could quickly emerge somewhere, start blasting, and disappear again in a flash. Perhaps Mock Duck's intimate knowledge of the tunnel system contributed to his aura of invincibility.

*Figure 17.3 The Wing Fat Shopping Arcade occupies part of a legendary tunnel in Chinatown*

*Figure 18.3  In Washington Heights, a long pedestrian tunnel connects to the subway*

In spite of such problems there is still a long passageway in Washington Heights that leads to the subway station at 191st Street. Although it is only used by pedestrians, it is officially registered as "Tunnel Street." At a depth of 17 stories, the station it leads to is the deepest one in the New York subway system and is usually accessed via elevators. The three-block-long tunnel saves subway riders from having to climb the hill to the top of the elevator shaft. In the early 1990s this tunnel was not necessarily a better option; it was littered with trash and drug paraphernalia, occasionally serving as an unofficial homeless shelter. Since then it has been renovated by the MTA.

*Figure 19.1 A handsomely deteriorated building at Seaview Hospital*

# CHAPTER NINETEEN

# The Tunnels of Seaview Hospital

Hospital tunnels fall into a special category of underground passages for the simple reason that they are strictly utilitarian and yet inherently creepy. The pleasure to be had from ruins is only skin deep, unless their still existing organs can be reassembled into a narrative, and this is usually possible in obsolete medical facilities. While the hospital may present a bright interior with sanitized surfaces, it will often have a squalid underbelly with neglected storage rooms, stain-ridden pathology labs, and dark passages to the morgue. The artifacts and equipment stored in these underground regions lend themselves to many interpretations, often infused with a morbid element.

Nearly all major hospitals have an intricate tunnel system that serves to distribute steam and other utilities, and provides a convenient way to move supplies, laundry, and, sometimes, the patients. These systems are usually just one story below ground, comprising a maze of seemingly endless tunnels unrelieved by windows or ventilation shafts. Most of these passages can only be accessed from within the hospital buildings and are never seen by the public while the facility is in use.

The abandoned structures of mental hospitals can be the destinations of particularly poignant visits. One of the city's prominent psychiatric centers, still very much in use, has a recently closed ward, whose basement area is filled with moldering patient clothing, medical equipment, and stacks of decaying mattresses. Furniture is stacked haphazardly inside dank, windowless rooms; small animal carcasses are left to rot on the floor. The tunnel entrances to this area bear signs proclaiming it a "shelter zone," and there is indeed evidence of at least one person residing here, albeit not in the sense intended by the hospital. If these subterranean regions are any indication of the patient wards, it does not bode well for the treatment of the mentally ill. For an active hospital, it is outrageously deteriorated—a sinister and depressing place.

*Figure 19.2 The tunnels and basements below one of the city's mental hospitals serve as decrepit storage areas*

In contrast, the ornate abandoned section of a once famous tuberculosis hospital on Staten Island tells a story of accomplishment: its success in curing the afflicted is what led to the demise of the facility. A large part of Seaview Hospital is still in use, but nearly all of the original buildings have been closed and now lie in ruins, including four large pavilions in the rear of the campus. Those pavilions are beautifully decrepit; their gaping windows reveal decaying interiors with gritty detritus and peeling paint.

When it was opened in 1913, Seaview Hospital had 1,100 beds and was focused on the treatment of tuberculosis, "the white plague," which at the time was the city's deadliest disease. This facility contributed greatly to the development of a vaccine in the early 1950s by conducting tests with a new antibiotic and effecting a major turnaround in terminal patients. This led to a decline in tuberculosis cases, which in turn resulted in a decrease in patients, and the hospital began to suffer financially. Although Seaview soon changed its primary function toward the care of the elderly, it was not feasible to maintain all the buildings.

Four of the eight pavilions, constructed between 1909 and 1911 in a mission revival style, were demolished in 1972 and replaced by a modern nursing facility that

*Figure 19.3  Seaview Hospital's terra cotta tiles are falling prey to the elements*

opened a year later. The state of the four remaining buildings has been addressed by preservationists and the Friends of Terra Cotta, a nonprofit organization interested in salvaging the unusual tile work on the upper levels of the wards. The original tiles were fabricated by the Dutch company Joost Thooft & Labouchere and are considered masterpieces of ceramic art. In beautiful detail, the terra cotta murals depict doctors, nurses, and patients interspersed with marine motifs, such as shells and ocean waves. Since sunlight and fresh air were considered crucial to the treatment of tuberculosis when the hospital opened, the pavilions offer much exposure to the elements, and their decor reflects their proximity to the waterfront.

All four pavilions are connected with each other through a long tunnel from which other passages branch off into adjacent buildings, linking most of the hospital campus. When I first visited this tunnel in the late 1990s, it had been raining, and a cool breeze rose from the black space, carrying the damp, foul, and slightly sweet smell of rotting

*Figure 19.4  A hallway inside one of the former women's wards at Seaview*

waste. From a staircase inside a middle pavilion, I emerged in the basement, which opened into the tunnel. The left side of the passage was brightly lit, whereas the right disappeared in darkness. It was a maintenance tunnel with a narrow walkway next to an impressive array of utility pipes. Although it was completely quiet, the string of lightbulbs was disconcerting, giving the impression that a door might open there at any moment. Nonetheless, I first headed toward the light.

Beyond the basement of another pavilion, a second tunnel branched off to the side. Here stood an old gurney that had obviously not been used in a very long time. This pedestrian tunnel was dimly illuminated by antiquated ceiling lamps and curved to the left, making it impossible to see its end. Its originally white walls had been thoroughly pierced with nails, which had since rusted, and in the orange light the rust stains gave the walls the appearance of having a skin

*Figure 19.5 A few of Seaview's buildings are connected by utility tunnels.*

disease. The tunnel seemed to head to the pathology building across the street from the pavilions. At the end of the passage was a set of double doors with lights behind them, signaling hospital activity, and I turned around. It was on the way back that I saw faint lettering on the wall, dated 1969: "To the Morgue." Beneath this was an arrow pointing to the direction I had just come from. This old gurney had probably transported more dead patients than live ones.

Now heading into the darker section of the tunnel, I realized I was going to end up in a large, outlying building that rose on an incline above the pavilions. The basement of this building had pitch-black, partially flooded rooms and was lined with tracks, which most likely were used for laundry carts. One of the windowless rooms had a dirty mattress on the floor and gave the impression that someone had resided here. Inside a flooded closet, on top of discolored debris, floated the arm of a plastic doll.

After resurfacing, I determined to come back soon to explore more sections of the eerie basements, but although a year passed until I returned, I was happy to find the gurney unmoved. Over the next several years, I detected no changes down here at all. A visit to this hospital was a kind of autopsy of a truly abandoned slice of New York. The many residents of this city who deplore its rapid modernization may be relieved to know that there are still a few locations, quietly preserved in the underground, where time has stood completely still.

*Figure 20.1  Columbia University has a large network of tunnels for utility distribution and pedestrian access*

# CHAPTER TWENTY

# The Labyrinth Below Columbia University

The basement of Columbia's philosophy building is brightly illumined even at night. At the bottom of an inconspicuous set of stairs lies a hallway filled with valves, steam pipes, instrument panels, and enigmatic machine parts. One night, after having made a spontaneous decision to unofficially explore Columbia's underground, my friend Steve Duncan and I found ourselves at the entrance of this hall, wondering where to begin. A door on our left concealed the book stacks beneath Low Library. To our right the steam pipes continued down the hallway, gracefully bending around a corner and out of sight. Both directions seemed interesting, but not nearly as tempting as the decrepit ladder in the back of the room. It led to a tiny hatch directly below the ceiling.

We quickly climbed up the ladder. Beyond the hatch we found a narrow, pitch-black corridor — a long steam tunnel providing an underground shortcut to the next building. Careful not to touch the hot steam pipes, we crept through the claustrophobic space along the masonry walls that seemed much older than the building we had started in. Just as the heat was becoming unbearable, the exit appeared in the beams of our flashlights. From the broken rungs of a ladder resting precariously against a web of rusted pipes, we ascended into the oldest part of the renowned university — the remnants of an insane asylum.

Columbia University, a world-famous center for education and research in the north of Manhattan, is recognized as one of the country's most prestigious universities. Lesser-known facts about the campus include that it was built on the former grounds of the Bloomingdale Insane Asylum and that it has one of the largest pedestrian tunnel systems in America.

Established in 1808, the Bloomingdale Asylum was one of the first psychiatric hospitals in the country, at a time when the priority in dealing with the mentally ill was generally not their treatment but their removal from society, even if this meant confining them in basement cells. The asylum initially occupied the basement of nearby New York Hospital, relocating to its own campus in Morningside Heights

*Figure 20.2 The Columbia University campus in 1907*

near 115th Street and Amsterdam Avenue in 1821. The area was still pastoral, its wilderness only sparsely dotted with settlements.

After the asylum was moved to Westchester in the 1890's, Seth Low, the president of Columbia University, became interested in the property the hospital had left behind. At that time the university was located in midtown Manhattan, but Low envisioned an entire academic village, erected in an architectural style reminiscent of the Italian renaissance. The campus at Morningside Heights suited him perfectly, even if nearly all of the existing buildings had to be demolished. Only Buell Hall, the original administration office, survived — and remains as the oldest structure on the Columbia campus today.

During the construction, many of Columbia's 71 buildings between Broadway and Amsterdam Avenue were connected by tunnels. After that of the Massachusetts Institute of Technology, Columbia's tunnel system is said to be the largest of any university in America and is probably the most famous.

The tunnels played a considerable role, for example, during the Manhattan Project, a US-based program to develop nuclear weapons in response to the Nazi threat in World War II. Even prior to the war, researchers at Columbia University achieved important breakthroughs in the area of nuclear science. This included the groundbreaking work of the Italian physicist Enrico Fermi, who researched radioactivity here. The results of the experiments inside Pupin Hall, Columbia's physics department, led to the first instance of nuclear fission in the United States.

*Figure 20.3  Buell Hall, formerly the Bloomingdale Insane Asylum's administration building,
is the only original hospital structure left on campus*

According to student accounts, the tunnels were used for the transport of the radioactive materials needed in the experiments. There are rumors of minor accidents and illnesses as a result of this transport, but facts and legends have always been interwoven in the tales of Columbia's underground. Eventually, the Manhattan Project moved to Chicago and finally Los Alamos. There, the bombs that later destroyed Hiroshima and Nagasaki were built.

The tunnels gained greater fame during another historic occurrence — the massive student protests of 1968. Students who had regularly used the tunnel system knew the layout fairly well, which became useful when thousands gathered to demonstrate against the Vietnam War. Many of them barricaded themselves on the campus for several days. Through the tunnels, students could move between buildings, collect supplies, and exchange information. However, they realized that if they could access the buildings through the subterranean passages, the police would be able to as well. The students erected as much of a blockade as possible, even though it was clear to everyone that the police would eventually gain the upper hand. One of the former protesters, Frank da Cruz, recently recalled the students' motives:

We made considerable efforts to barricade the tunnel entrances to our buildings, forcing the police to come in the front door where all the world could watch. If they used the tunnels to come in and take us out, nobody would have seen them and they might have applied their nightsticks and flashlights with considerably more vigor, nor would the world have been treated to all those famous photos and films.

This proved an effective plan because when the police did finally break through, the media accompanied them. *Time*, *Life*, and many other publications showed dramatic photos of bloody students.

After the 1960s, the university administration sealed off the tunnels. Of course, a few unsecured doors and other possible entryways always remained. Students continued to seek out the passageways, less for the shortcuts between buildings, but more because they became curious about the legends and history of Columbia's underground. Starting in the early 90s, the exploration of college tunnels among students — sometimes referred to as "vadding" — became an increasingly popular pastime nationwide, fueled by online newsgroup exchanges. Due to their length and history, Columbia's tunnels have since gained special status among adventurous students.

The most intriguing questions in recent years concerned the Manhattan Project and the cyclotron, which was used to split an atom for the first time, and the remains of which are still stored there. One student, who claimed to have stolen spent uranium from the basement of Pupin Hall, became a popular subject of speculation. "The way I heard the story," wrote a fellow student named Adam, "was that investigators [ ... ] were hunting around with Geiger counters and something registered right by his roommate's bed — he didn't seem to get along with his roommate too well. They found uranium planted in his alarm clock!"

These and other tales about discoveries in the university tunnels tend to amuse the former Columbia student Steve Duncan, who has explored and mapped the tunnel system in great detail, which came in handy during our mutual expedition. When we surfaced into the former basement of the old mental hospital, the lights near the steam pipes at the tunnel exit were the only source of illumination; the cellar and its narrow hallways lay in darkness. Steve and I decided to head into opposite directions, something I regretted as soon as a large rat darted into the beam of my flashlight.

Circling the basement, I could see traces of where the building had been shifted from its foundation. The original supports were still poking out from the ground, and pieces of old bricks were scattered in the corners. But it was the small chunk of plaster that Steve handed me when we met up that really evoked the

*Figure 20.4 The basement beneath Buell Hall is the oldest underground structure accessible through Columbia's tunnels*

building's age. Thick black hairs stuck out from the brittle wedge — horse hairs, which had once been popular to use for increased support.

This, the only remaining cellar from the Bloomingdale Asylum, seemed to have remained untouched in the last decades. Only the steam pipes, tagged with the labels "asbestos-free insulation," indicated that anyone had been here recently. When I remarked on the lack of graffiti, Steve explained, "Most Columbia students are geeks. They have no sense for graffiti. The only writing you might find here are quotes from J.R.R. Tolkien."

After returning to the philosophy building past the hot steam pipes, we soon found ourselves in a vast labyrinth of tunnels. The subterranean corridors continually led to intersections that promised great varieties of scenery ahead — old masonry vaults, futuristic chambers with steel pipes, sparkling aluminum

*Figure 20.5  A hatch provides access between steam tunnels*

insulation, cubbyholes white with moist steam, passages lined with brightly colored valves and conduits, and dimly lit corridors where water had collected in puddles.

It was an odd sensation to move through these dark spaces, crouching past clusters of utility pipes, only to emerge into a public part of the university. At one point we opened a door into a cafeteria where students were drinking coffee, feeling like cave spelunkers unexpectedly stumbling into civilization. The two young women across from me seemed somewhat perplexed by my mud-stained coat and flashlight, but it was nice to be able to buy a bottle of water from a vending machine before plunging back into the tunnels.

Most impressive was the basement below the university's power plant. Here the machines, reminiscent of those in Fritz Lang's film *Metropolis*, seemed to have taken on a life of their own. There was no caretaker in sight. The instruments

*Figure 20.6  The tunnel leading to the power plant is partially flooded*

hissed, groaned, and spouted steam from all corners. In contrast, the old masonry hallways in the sub-basement of this building were an oasis of calm. Tracks, once used during coal transport, were partially buried in the muddy floor. Wheelbarrows and machine parts lay in desolate corners, collecting dust.

Before exiting the labyrinth of tunnels, we passed a hallway whose walls were densely tagged. Here were also the Tolkien quotes Steve had mentioned. Wasn't it a bit far-fetched to compare our odyssey through Columbia's tunnels with a journey through the mines of Moria? Steve read the quotes and shook his head, smiling. But when we surfaced back onto the street, he did seem pleased to have returned safely from the nether worlds once more.

Figure 21.1 *The Water Battery at Fort Totten, now a ruin, was constructed in the 1860s*

Figure 21.1B *The entrance to an abandoned ammunitions magazine at Fort Tilden
on Rockaway Beach*

# CHAPTER TWENTY-ONE

# The Graffiti of Dead Soldiers

Jutting out from the northern edge of Queens into the Long Island Sound, Fort Totten seems to be at the edge of the world. The two nineteenth-century mine casings flanking its security gate presage an unexpected entry into another era, a journey toward one of the most impressive ruins in New York.

Built in the 1860s to protect the city from an invasion through its back door, the Long Island Sound, the campus is only partly used by the army today. Many of the buildings are rented out to various agencies, such as the Coast Guard, an NYPD canine training unit, and an ambulance driver school. Yet in the back of this complex, behind a dilapidated fence, sits the abandoned historic section of the fort, an assemblage of blanched, decrepit shells. This is the heart of what was once intended to be the most powerful military base in the state of New York.

New York's forts tend to be largely forgotten today, and yet their remnants lie all over the city. The most high-profile fortifications are in the Battery in lower Manhattan, Fort Tryon in Inwood, and the two military bases on each side of the Verrazano Bridge. Some of the abandoned sites—such as on Hart Island or Governors Island—are not usually accessible, whereas Fort Tilden on Rockaway Beach has become part of a dune landscape, inviting solitary walks among the partially buried bunkers. During the Cold War, Fort Tilden and several other locations in the metropolitan area housed Nike Missile batteries, whose launchers were based in underground installations.

The city's original army points were constructed primarily to fend off invasions by the British. When the British forces departed New York in 1783, the need to protect the city's vulnerable waterfronts against future attacks became increasingly critical. In the early nineteenth century, a young military engineer by the name of Joseph G. Totten assisted in the design of several of the city's forts, making crucial innovations. Most importantly, he improved the design of casemate systems, which meant that rather than

*Figure 21.2  A tunnel connects the seaside battery to a series of underground bunkers*

relying on cannons on top of the batteries, the forts' main firepower came from weapons placed behind narrow windows on several building levels.

Recognizing the vulnerability of the Long Island Sound, Totten planned to fortify the army grounds at Willets Point, where the sound meets the East River. In 1862, when the Civil War again brought the city's need for strong military bases to the forefront, construction began on a large battery facing the water, which was intended to have five levels of casemates and granite walls with a thickness of eight feet. But the plans were modified at the end of the Civil War, since such a massive structure was now considered too extravagant. When its construction was halted a few years later, after utilizing about 15,000 blocks of granite, the water battery had only two tiers of casemates and the upper level was left without a roof. That is how it remains to this day.

Soon after the Civil War, army engineers based in a laboratory at the Willets Point site began conducting substantial experiments with submarine mines and torpedoes, some of which could be detonated through electrical cables that unreeled as the devices were propelled underwater. The subaquatic minefield stretched to Fort Schuyler, which had been built in the 1830s on the Bronx shore across Willets Point.

*Figure 21.3 Stalactites inside the derelict bunkers.*

In 1898 the fort was officially named after Joseph Totten, but its military use began to decline. The entire mortar battery, considered obsolete by the 1930s, was filled in and buried beneath a field. The army gradually abandoned the base and since the late 1960s, the military has used it primarily for housing purposes and the 77th Army Reserve Command. The property currently awaits a transfer to the Parks Department, which may significantly transform the ruins from their present condition.

In their current state of abandonment, the ruins are striking. The old fort still contains the water battery, bunkers, and underground storage vaults for mines and ammunitions. Rising up from the water to the east of the Throgs Neck Bridge, the battery is a formidable architectural relic. Overgrown with weeds, its mortarless granite arches rising gracefully from the upper story, it seems incongruously peaceful.

A small portico inside the west foundation wall of the battery has been broken through to reveal an old flooded tunnel, which runs from the hill behind the battery toward the seawall. Andy Hogger, my informal guide on an expedition to these ruins, tells me that this passage may be the remnant of an attempt to tunnel to Fort Schuyler. (During the 1890s there were apparently plans for an underwater tunnel between the two forts along the minefield.)

Military sites are good fodder for tales of secret tunnels, since they are easily embellished with accounts of sinister experiments and difficult to verify. There are rumors of a subaquatic tunnel between Fort Wadsworth on Staten Island and Fort Hamilton in Brooklyn, running roughly parallel to the Verrazano Bridge. During a search for the abandoned shafts of another tunnel from Bay Ridge to Staten Island, planned by John Hylan in the 1920s but never finished, I had met a park ranger who claimed to have seen the entrance of the military tunnel on Staten Island and described it as "big enough to drive a truck through." Whether it exists

*Figure 21.4 The entrance to a tunnel that may have been intended to connect to Fort Schuyler beneath the Long Island Sound*

or not, it would have made sense for the army to have a hidden subterranean connection between Brooklyn and Staten Island in case of attack.

The tunnel at Fort Totten is very narrow, which lends credibility to the theory that it was designed merely to contain and service the electrical cables that controlled the mines beneath the Long Island Sound. Fort Schuyler, now part of a college campus, has a corresponding tunnel segment that also terminates at the seawall. While standing inside this small brick-lined corridor, however, my ruminations are interrupted by a more immediate concern. In all my time spent in New York tunnels, this is my first encounter with cave crickets. They are big and nasty-looking, and stirred up by the flashlight, they begin jumping recklessly between the wet walls. I have to hightail it out of there. Give me a Grand Central rat any day of the week—I'm not equipped for an onslaught of something that actually occurs in nature.

Back outside, another tunnel entrance awaits. This one welcomes me with the graffiti "Go back out lady, this is a hoar house." If *only* there were whores here—at least they would keep out the crickets. Here, as Andy helpfully points out,

*Figure 21.5  Soldiers began etching their names into the tunnel walls in the late ninetenth century*

the insects roam in packs across the white walls. Luckily the underground rooms beyond—once used to store munitions—offer a safe distance from the walls. The barren rooms lie beneath the hill that separates the main campus of Fort Totten from the battery. Also running beneath the hill is a large pedestrian passage, the most interesting part of the site.

This tunnel is one of the oldest surviving pedestrian tunnels in New York. The 500-foot-long passage connects the nine subterranean bunkers in the front of the historic campus to the seaside battery. What makes it interesting is that soldiers began leaving their marks on the walls more than a hundred years ago. The names and dates etched into the walls range back to 1896.

Looming in large yellow letters next to the names are the words "Remember the Maine." The Maine was an American battleship that had blown up in the waters outside of Havana, Cuba, in 1898, causing more than 200 fatalities. The battle cry "Remember the Maine" could be heard all over the country as the Spanish-American War ensued. It was in preparation for this war that the mines were planted between Fort Totten and Fort Schuyler.

It is hard to tell how old this particular graffiti is, but it brings the history of the fort to life, imparting vitality to the narrow tunnel by the seawall as much as the mine casings flanking the fort's entrance. It will be interesting to see whether the old soldier tags in this tunnel will remain untouched if this passage is opened to the public some day.

part VI  Building Foundations

*Figure 22.1 After the terror attacks on 9/11, entrances to damaged subway stations were temporarily sealed with plywood*

CHAPTER TWENTY-TWO

# New York's Largest Foundation

On the morning of September 11, 2001, someone we will call "Elliott" was on his way to work in midtown Manhattan. When he got on a number 4 train from Brooklyn, he already knew that a plane had crashed into one of the towers of the World Trade Center and was not surprised to hear an announcement that the train would bypass Fulton Street because of earlier incidents.

His train had just departed the Wall Street station and was almost directly below the World Trade Center when the first tower collapsed. "Everyone on the train noticed a change in the air pressure—ears popping and doors moving slightly in their frames," Elliott recalled later. No one knew what had happened, but moments later the emergency brakes were activated, and with a panicked voice the conductor announced, "Everyone to the front of the train, now, to evacuate!" Elliott, who was in the last car, had just begun moving when another announcement came: everyone was directed to go to the rear instead, since there was smoke heading toward the front.

"I got to the rear storm door and looked out into the tunnel; there was what looked like smoke starting to roll in from that side too, and the tunnel lights were out." The train operator had arrived in the last car, saw the smoke, cursed, and called control to receive further instructions. But control was busy. "He kept on calling, saying he had a five-minute situation, and where the fuck was the assistance he had been promised 15 minutes ago—he needed someone to come and open up the Fulton station so he could evacuate." Instead he was told to reverse the train and let everyone out at Wall Street.

However, in order to move the train from the rear, the operator had to get the brake handle from the front car, which he didn't think was a good idea, since the passengers were beginning to panic. Just then, an MTA worker with a mask and flashlight came down the tracks toward them and retrieved the brake handle from the front. Yet the train could barely make progress toward Wall Street. Because there was no power to any of the signals, the trippers, which are installed along the tracks to stop subway trains in case of emergency, had been activated, and it was a slow, bumpy ride back toward Wall Street.

As soon as the first car had reached the platform, the operator keyed open a door in the station and told everyone to get out fast. "We ran through the station, which was pretty smoky and had a layer of dust on the ground," Elliott recounts. "No one really knew what was going on." They emerged into darkness; the dust and swirling debris on the street made it impossible to see anything. "People kept yelling, 'When are we going to go out?'—It was so dark, they didn't realize they were already out on the street." Someone shouted directions to get inside a building. Only when he had reached shelter did Elliott hear that one of the towers had collapsed.

Soon the news about the terrorist attacks on the twin towers had made headlines around the world. Almost 2,800 people were killed and more than 20 buildings were destroyed or damaged in New York. Miraculously, large parts of the trade center foundation had survived almost intact. But nearly a century of skyscraper history had preceded the World Trade Center, and through trial and error, the technology of constructing solid foundations had evolved as well.

*Figure 22.2  A photo of damaged structural supports, taken by the foundation engineer George Tamaro Jr. shortly after the attacks*

*Mattresses are piled in deteriorating heaps in the basement of a mental hospital*

*Long after its last transport, a gurney remains in a tunnel at Seaview Hospital.*

*Remnants of the cyclotron at Columbia University*

*The Water Battery at Fort Totten*

*This tunnel at Fort Totten ends abruptly against the seawall*

*Cortlandt Street Station was severely damaged during the terror attacks on 9/11*

*Inside the Brooklyn Bridge anchorage in Brooklyn*

*The vaults below Old St. Patrick's Cathedral date back to the mid-nineteenth century*

*The central aisle of the crypt beneath Old St. Patrick's Cathedral*

*Figure 22.3  The Woolworth Building, once the city's tallest structure, is supported by 120-foot-deep concrete pillars*

New York is known as the ultimate city of skyscrapers, but someone looking up at a tall building may not consider the other end of the vertical expanse, and how much has to be put in motion in the underground for the building to function at all. High-rises need to be anchored solidly in the ground, which in New York means that engineers have to locate bedrock before anything can go up. In the financial district, where the city's first tall buildings rose, the schist is buried below landfill and other obstacles, such as rocks, old foundations, and decayed wood. Further north, the bedrock often lies close to the surface, such as at Rockefeller Center, where it was found 10 feet below the street and had to be blasted to make room for the basement levels.

Additionally, skyscrapers need to be furnished with all manner of utility equipment. An article titled "Underground New York" that appeared in the magazine *Technical World* in 1905 lists the machinery inside the basement of a typical office building on Nassau Street in the beginning of the twentieth century: "On the fourth subfloor of this building, 33 feet below mean tide water, are eight great boilers aggregating over 3,000 horsepower; a 10-ton ice machine; 15 pumps for house, fire, elevator, and boiler-feeding use; 3 electric machines; 2 great feed-water heaters; engines; dynamos; an electric ventilating apparatus; automatic sewage ejectors; and ash-lifts."

The invention of the elevator made the construction of tall buildings a desirable option in the crowded financial district as early as the 1860s and by 1875, the Western Union Building was only one of several buildings ten stories tall. The Pulitzer Building, which opened in 1890 and surpassed 300 feet, had a basement with enough space to store 500 tons of paper, in addition to a generating plant in a vault below the sidewalk.

Toward the end of the nineteenth century, the competition for the city's tallest building began in earnest. Cast iron columns enabled the construction of more stories on a smaller foundation. The Manhattan Life Building on Broadway was the first skyscraper whose foundation rested on pneumatic caissons, which supported the building's piers on bedrock nearly 60 feet below street level. North of the Financial District, the Flatiron Building marked Manhattan's skyline in 1902; the Times Tower appeared in 1904.

The construction of the neogothic Woolworth Building on Broadway required some technical innovations. While the groundwater in this area was at 35 feet below the surface, the bedrock lay about 120 feet deep. With the aid of pneumatic caissons, 69 concrete pillars had to be sunk into the ground to support the steel columns of the building. At 792 feet, with a swimming pool and restaurant in its basement and gargoyles on its roof, all aspects of the building were beautifully detailed. This "Cathedral of Commerce" was the city's tallest structure until 1930.

The race for the city's grandest skyscraper came to a head when the Chrysler and Empire State buildings were erected. The Chrysler Building, at a height of 1,046 feet, won the competition for only four months, until the Empire State Building

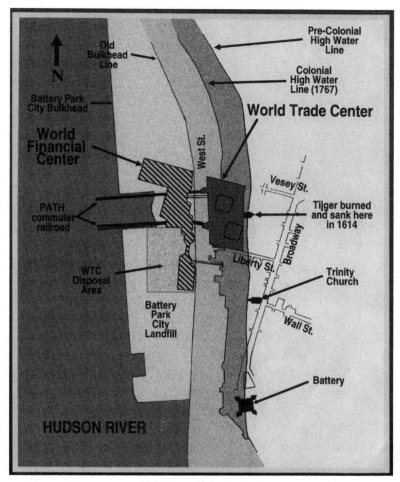

*Figure 22.4  A map by the engineering firm Mueser Rutledge, showing changes along the waterfront at the World Trade Center site*

surpassed it in 1931 with a height of 1,250 feet. Until the construction of the World Trade Center, it remained the city's tallest. Before the Empire State Building site could be excavated, the original Waldorf-Astoria Hotel had to be demolished and an underground stream had to be diverted from the site. The 365,000-ton building rests on solid bedrock 55 feet beneath the street.

"Some foundations, like those of the Empire State Building, are so routine they aren't interesting," the foundation expert Robert White told a reporter for *The New Yorker* during an inspection of the largest construction site in the city's history. "A one-story service station built on a swamp could be more exciting. But on this kind of filled land there is nothing but trouble."

The land he was referring to was a large parcel on the west side of lower Manhattan, which had been acquired by the Port Authority of New York. By the early 1960s, the city was economically depressed, the crime rate was high, and the mood pessimistic. Against this backdrop the Port Authority was planning a momentous urban renewal project, which included what would become the world's tallest buildings. The plot of land contained not only numerous decrepit houses but also the old Hudson & Manhattan Terminal, now the Port Authority's headquarters. Along with 163 other buildings, the terminal would have to make way for the World Trade Center.

The plan was to construct a complex of seven buildings in an area measuring 16 acres, including twin towers with a skeleton of load-bearing steel, rising 110 stories each. In its negotiations with the city, the Port Authority had agreed to enlarge the southern tip of Manhattan by 24 acres by depositing the soil excavated from the site into a cofferdam in the Hudson River. Much of the lower Manhattan

*Figure 22.5 Preparing the Trade Center site for new construction after 9/11*

waterfront area, including the World Trade Center site, rested on similarly created landfill.

While the first houses were demolished on Dey Street in March 1966, engineers were tackling the question of how to anchor two giant towers inside a loosely filled parcel of land that had been part of the river only a few centuries before. The bedrock, which lay up to 80 feet below the street, would not only have to support a weight of 1.5 million tons, but it would also have to keep out the groundwater. How to prevent the Hudson from continually flooding the construction site was a major concern, since pumping out such large volumes of water was not feasible. It was decided to construct an underground barrier around the entire site, which would henceforth be nicknamed the "bathtub."

A three-foot-wide trench was constructed, consisting of adjacent segments, 22 feet long and 7 stories deep. The trench ran along the site's perimeter, and to help it retain its shape, it was temporarily filled with a mixture of bentonite and water. Then, a steel cage was inserted into each segment, which was filled with concrete that pushed the lighter bentonite mixture back to the surface where it was removed. Over the next 14 months, the 158 individual sections of the bathtub were completed. Now the real excavations could begin. A large receptacle fashioned from steel

*Figure 22.6 A PATH tube is peeled from the underground during the initial excavation of the WTC site*

cofferdams was constructed along the waterfront to receive 1.2 million cubic yards of soil, filling a 6-block area 700 feet from the shore into the Hudson. It was here that Battery Park City would rise.

As the landfill was transferred from the bathtub to the river site, all the utility lines traversing the construction site had to be diverted. To stop the bathtub walls from caving in toward the pit, they had to be held in place by anchors secured in the rock outside the foundation—a complicated undertaking calling for considerable ingenuity by the engineers. Yet another challenge was posed by the tubes of the old H&M railroad—the PATH trains ran directly through the site, transporting 80,000 riders between New Jersey and Manhattan every day. Since it was out of the question to suspend the service, the tunnels had to be artificially supported while the soil was excavated around them.

The sight of the old tubes suddenly being peeled from the soil must have been very strange. Since the turn of the century, they had been buried; now the workers were carving them out like fossils, supporting them on steel beams. The metal that the tunnels were constructed of expanded in the sunlight, so the cylinders were sliced open on the sides to keep them from developing dangerous tears. But after a train operator slammed on the brakes at the sudden sight of a sunbeam on the tracks, the slits were covered with metal. Most passengers were not even aware of this unusual section of their journey.

The excavations yielded many relics from the past: coins, dishes, bottles, cannonballs, a time capsule from 1884, and shredded shoes, which could be worn on either the left or right foot (which, according to archaeologists, dated the shoes to a time before 1865). The removal of a large anchor required 19 men. It later found its final resting place on the sixth basement level of the Trade Center. What remained elusive was any trace of the Tijger, the ship that had been partially unearthed during the construction of the Cortlandt Street station.

Regardless of their aesthetic merit, the completed twin towers could not help but impress. At a height of 1,362 and 1,368 feet, they were the tallest buildings in the world. Around 430 companies and 50,000 employees would ultimately occupy the site, which was inaugurated in April 1973. The basement areas were massive, taking up nearly as much square footage as the Empire State Building. It was seven stories deep, containing large parking facilities, retail areas, pedestrian passages, and new PATH and subway stations. The deepest restaurant was the Commuters Cafe, five levels below the street at the entrance to the PATH train.

The Trade Center's underground maintenance areas contained trash facilities, truck ramps, abandoned PATH tracks, and the Operations Control Center, which

*Figure 22.7  Ground Zero in October 2001*

provided security services from beneath the south tower. On the fifth basement levels between the two towers lay the entire air conditioning unit inside a three-story tall subterranean hall, fed by water from the Hudson. There were also little-publicized underground storage spaces, such as bank vaults containing gold and other precious metals. And in the basement of World Trade Center Six, the CIA had stored contraband, including drugs and weapons.

When the towers collapsed on September 11, 2001, New York's physical and spiritual makeup was irrevocably changed. The subterranean topography of downtown Manhattan was completely altered. The force with which the buildings crashed down shook the underground so severely that not only the three-foot-thick bathtub wall, but the tunnels and foundations in the entire vicinity, felt the tremors.

In the first few days after the attack, as the rescue workers tackled the red-hot metal heaps that towered up to 60 feet high, news of underground discoveries came to light. There were entire sections of the subterranean areas that had apparently survived the attacks. Like cave spelunkers, several firefighters, engineers, and cops had carefully made their way into the lower depths of the foundation, initially in the hope to find survivors. They found neither dead nor living, but an entire ghost world opened up to them instead.

In an article for the *New York Times*, James Glanz likened the scene to "the unreal city of T.S. Eliot's *The Waste Land*, a place where dread lurks in the shadows and terrible things emerge by gleam of light." The stores, now lying in pitch darkness, had been left open. Credit cards still lay next to the cash registers, and half-eaten bagels waited on plates while the shelves were stocked with wilting produce. One photo that surfaced from this underworld was particularly haunting: a large Bugs Bunny figure that seemed monstrous in the glare of the artificial light.

It was also eerie to take the subway past damaged stations for some time afterward. Many underground areas that had bustled with life one moment now

*Figure 22.8 The temporary WTC PATH station opened in November 2003*

evoked silent dread. "Don't stop here," said the hand written signs posted at the damaged Cortlandt Street station, which the N and R trains passed by as soon as the line was opened again a few weeks later. The lights in the station remained dim as if it too were in mourning. For some time after the World Trade Center stop on the E line reopened, it remained desolate. The station's name had been blackened out on the large signs hanging outside the platforms.

Mike Donnelly, an ironworker from Local 40 who was working in the pit in the first days after the attacks, decided on an impulse to visit the other Cortlandt Street station, which lay in ruins after being destroyed beneath the debris. He moved aside the pieces of plywood barring the station's entrance and, with the aid of a flashlight, walked down to the platform. He jumped onto the tracks, heading into the destruction area, which was dark and covered in thick dust. "It was like Armageddon," Mike said afterward. The firefighters who had come right after the attacks had written on the walls in orange paint, indicating that no bodies had been found here. On the side of the staircase, Mike also saw a tag by the old-school graffiti writer Stay High 149, which marked the experience for him.

*Figure 22.9 Having withstood the terror attacks, the bathtub will remain at least partially visible in the new WTC site design*

"He represented the beginning, among all the devastation that was the end," Mike said. "That made an impact."

The destroyed station was cleared away by spring 2002, while the MTA began to build a new structure with tunnels that could be integrated into the 1 and 9 lines. Service along this route resumed one year after the attacks, with the trains passing the unfinished platforms, which will be completed in conjunction with the construction of the new buildings at Ground Zero.

The PATH service from lower Manhattan to New Jersey had to be put on hold for more than two years. Shortly after the attacks, the tracks of the Exchange Place station in New Jersey were getting flooded with water from Ground Zero, primarily from the burst water pipes. To prevent the entire system from flooding, both tubes were quickly sealed with concrete plugs on the New Jersey side (but not before a few cops had the enviable opportunity to take a raft through the tubes toward Manhattan to see the extent of the damage). Below the World Trade Center, one empty PATH train had been left standing inside the station, three of its cars crushed.

A temporary PATH station opened at the World Trade Center site in November 2003 and has quickly become the busiest station in the system. In a few years it will be replaced by an inspired permanent structure designed by Santiago Calatrava, with two large glass wings that will open on each anniversary of the terrorist attacks. A glass roof will allow sunlight to illuminate the platforms 60 feet underground.

The transportation hub evolving at Ground Zero will likely be formidable, since the plans include not only the new PATH station, but access to 14 subway lines, people movers and pedestrian tunnels, and a link to the LIRR and JFK International Airport. One of the plans currently under discussion involves building a new tunnel from downtown to the LIRR station on Atlantic Avenue. Another proposal, which is opposed by a number of Battery Park residents, entails burying a section of West Street inside a tunnel and building a promenade on its roof. The construction of the transportation facilities will likely not be finished until 2009.

The rebuilt World Trade Center site will also have public underground elements. As it stands now, the memorial to those killed in the attacks on 9/11 will include a subterranean interpretive center to provide a context for the tragic events of that day. It will also contain an underground chamber below the footprints of the north tower that will hold the nearly 20,000 pieces of unidentified human remains.

The bathtub, which made the World Trade Center possible in the first place, may be reinforced by additional supports, but it will continue to embrace the site. In his original plans for the new building complex, the architect Daniel Libeskind had specified that the slurry walls should remain visible for 30 feet before entering the ground. While the plans for the site will likely continue to evolve, it seems probable that the bathtub will at least partially remain exposed, allowing future generations to marvel at this masterpiece of engineering.

*Figure 23.1  Inside the Brooklyn Bridge anchorage in Brooklyn, which until 9/11 was used as a performance and exhibition space by Creative Time*

# CHAPTER TWENTY-THREE

# Unusual Foundations

In New York City, difficult building excavations are the rule, and the engineering annals are filled with stories of complications caused by geological quirks. But subterranean streams and quicksand are not the only things lending flavor to the city's foundations. There are also a number of buildings whose underground origins are notable for more historic reasons. The sections below focus on three structures that evolved from unusual underground constructions: the Brooklyn Bridge, the New York Public Library, and the American Museum of Natural History.

## THE BROOKLYN BRIDGE

Like the basement of an old castle, the masonry vault stretches into the darkness. Its windowless spaces are cool and musty, making this an ideal area to store wine year-round. While the structure may conjure up the drawings of imaginary prisons by Giovanni Piranesi, its purpose is far from sinister—it is part of the anchorage of the Brooklyn Bridge.

Before the bridge was erected, Brooklyn and Manhattan were connected only by ferry service, which was unreliable in bad weather. Albany had given the green light to a bridge construction across the East River back in 1802, yet the proposed plans were unrealistic and risky, since the local engineers lacked the experience for such a tremendous project. When the Wheeling Bridge across the Ohio River collapsed during a severe storm in 1854, there was even more reluctance to build a suspension bridge in New York. Although the ferries had contributed to Brooklyn's rapid growth into a desirable residential area, they could not keep up with the city's transportation demands, and frustrated New Yorkers joked that it was faster to get to Albany than to Brooklyn.

The engineer John Roebling, who had emigrated from Germany in 1831, had built a few small but solid suspension bridges in Pennsylvania and Ohio, and saw a possible

*Figure 23.2 The Brooklyn Bridge in 2003*

solution to the problems of such a complex river crossing. In 1867 he submitted a proposal for a bridge that was not suspended by rope, as was customary, but by braided steel cables. His design was accepted and in 1870 the construction began.

Because the bed of the East River consisted of unpredictable layers of soil and rocks, the bridge towers had to be built on top of caissons—huge, waterproof boxes made of wood and reinforced with a metal frame, each about half the size of a city block. The Brooklyn caisson, which was installed first, was towed down the East River by tug boats in a brief public appearance before disappearing forever at the river bottom. These boxes, which were open at the bottom, were sunk into the river like diving bells, so the construction of the towers could be started on their roofs. As the towers began to rise, increasing the pressure, the caissons were gradually forced deeper into the riverbed. The rocks and mud that were pushed up from the ground had to continuously be cleared out by a work crew, laboring in several of the claustrophobic compartments of the caisson.

The roofs of the caissons were prevented from collapsing from the weight of the towers by raised air pressure, and the working conditions were hellish. A reporter for *Harper's Magazine*, who accompanied the workers into one of the

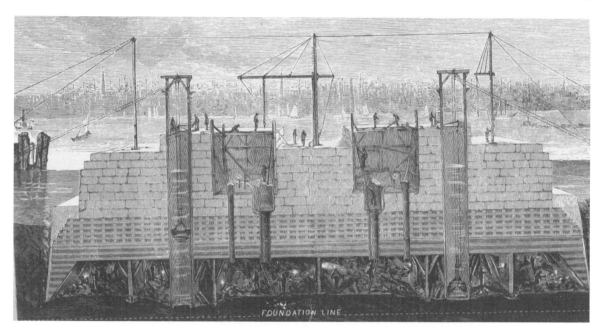

*Figure 23.3 Men at work inside the Brooklyn caisson in 1870*

dark, wet chambers, compared the airlock to a large jar, only sufficient for a dozen men to stand "like meats for preservation." The already difficult excavation work was hindered by blowouts and other mishaps. Altogether, the construction was estimated to have cost 40 lives. John Roebling died of tetanus in 1869 before the first tower was erected. His son, Washington Roebling, who subsequently took over, fell victim to the bends and had to direct the construction from his bed with the assistance of his wife Emily.

The opening of the bridge on May 24, 1883, was one of New York's greatest public celebrations. Tens of thousands of people assembled around what had become the largest suspension bridge in the world, crowding to hear the speech by Mayor Abram Hewitt, who described it as a monument to the "moral qualities of the human soul." With the exception of Trinity Church, the bridge towers were the tallest structures in New York.

The approaches to the bridge, and the vaults beneath them, were designed differently on each side of the river. Driving across toward the west affords a great view of the Manhattan anchorage, which is connected to the vaults below the approach by an arch. Most of the windows of these tremendous structures have been sealed, although a few still offer a glimpse at the dark chambers inside. Throughout the twentieth century, the rooms served a multitude of functions, including being rented out as wine cellars or work areas for carpenters and welders.

*Figure 23.4  Beneath the Manhattan approach to the Brooklyn Bridge*

Until the mid-1990s some of these areas were also being used by the homeless. In 1994, after a fire had broken out in one of the rooms, the police made a concentrated effort to drive out the underground residents, which numbered around 50. After confiscating the mattresses, TVs, and other furniture inside the anchorage, city authorities sealed many of the windows. As part of an unfinished, long obsolete project to bring subway service across the Brooklyn Bridge, there is still a connection between the anchorage and a subway tunnel, but with the increased security, it is unlikely to be used much by the homeless at this time.

The anchorage on the Brooklyn side has been well maintained, thanks to the efforts of Creative Time, an artistic group that has organized cultural events inside the unique space since the 1980s. Unfortunately, as a result of the security measures since 9/11, no one is able to organize events there any longer. Hopefully the public will be able to enjoy the anchorage again before too long.

*Figure 23.5  An entrance to the vaults inside the Manhattan anchorage of the Brooklyn Bridge*

## THE NEW YORK PUBLIC LIBRARY

The Murray Hill Reservoir, which rose at the corner of Fifth Avenue and 42nd Street with all the somberness of an Egyptian temple, must have been an impressive sight. The retaining walls, 44 feet high and 25 feet wide, held the water from the Croton Aqueduct in two massive rectangular tanks. By means of staircases inside the walls, it was possible to climb up to the parapet and stroll around the reservoir's perimeter, and many New Yorkers took advantage of this opportunity to enjoy the city views.

Some pieces of this reservoir are still buried beneath the main building of the New York Public Library. In 1899, the obsolete tanks were demolished to make way for a new Beaux-Arts library building, designed by the architects John Carrere and Thomas Hastings and financed by the estate of Governor Samuel Tilden. The construction started in 1902, and when the library was opened in 1911, the building was the largest marble structure in the country.

*Figure 23.6 Beneath Bryant Park is a vast storage space for the library's book collection*

On the day of the library's inauguration, more than one million catalogued books were ready to be pulled from the stacks inside seven basement levels within a half hour of being requested. This speedy delivery is still the pride of the library. But by 1965, when the stacks, with more than 88 miles of shelf space, were filled to the bursting point, another storage space had to be found. Nothing seemed more logical than utilizing the underground area below Bryant Park directly behind the library.

Bryant Park had already undergone many changes. In the beginning of the nineteenth century it was used as a cemetery for many victims of the yellow fever epidemic in 1798; when the potter's field at Washington Square was cleared out, the coffins ended up there. In 1853, the park, now called Reservoir Square, had a brief moment of glory when the Crystal Palace was erected there and it became the site of the country' first World's Fair. However, the beautiful steel and glass structure was destroyed by a fire only five years later.

The plot of land was named Bryant Park in 1884, but was not landscaped in its present state until 1934. By the late 1970s, the park had increasingly become a meeting point for drug dealers and the homeless, serving, among other things, as a kind of backyard to the people living in the tunnels of nearby Grand Central

Terminal. But in the 1990s, the park area was rehabilitated. It is now used for fashion shows, outdoor film screenings, and other cultural functions.

Before Bryant Park received its facelift, the excavations for the library's new storage space began, which included a 120-foot-long tunnel to connect the new underground stacks with the library. In the course of the construction, an increasing amount of remnants from the old reservoir began to surface. The contractors also had to work around the subway tunnel for the 7 train, which enters a slight curve near Sixth Avenue next to the underground storehouse. To protect the subway from any shock waves created during the blasting, workers drilled a series of holes into the adjacent bedrock, creating a buffer of air pockets.

In 1991, the new subterranean warehouse, with 120,000 square feet of stacks and equipped with movable shelves, was ready for service. One special chamber, whose location the library does not want to reveal and which is heavily secured, contains its most valuable possessions: George Washington's diary, Thomas Jefferson's personal accounts, rare manuscripts by Herman Melville, and other irreplaceable materials.

The library's most recent construction project paid particular attention to its historic foundation. In the summer of 2002, the South Court opened, a new building in one of the two inner courtyards. Since the library's opening, not much had ever changed in this court. For a long time it still contained a well from which horses used to drink. When the site was excavated for the new building addition, pieces of the old reservoir walls were found and integrated into the basement. They can now be seen publicly from a few vantage points inside the building. The contractors also came across another foundation wall, which, according to the consulting archaeologists, could be even older than the Croton Aqueduct.

## DINOSAURS IN CENTRAL PARK

In 1854, the Crystal Palace in London organized an exhibition in Sydenham Park that caused a stir all the way to New York. It consisted of a display of artificial dinosaur models at a time when very little was known about the actual shape of these prehistoric creatures. New York coveted the dinosaurs, and the Central Park Commission decided to tap the resources of the creator of the models, Benjamin Waterhouse Hawkins.

The construction of Central Park was under way by the 1860s, and about sixty acres on its west side had been set aside for a new museum. Hawkins's success in London had inspired the Central Park Commission to plan a similarly large diorama, which would extend into the underground in a series of catacombs. This new Paleozoic Museum was to exhibit prehistoric animals that once roamed on American soil. In 1868 the foundation of the museum was excavated inside the park near 63rd Street and today's Tavern on the Green.

That same year Hawkins, who had agreed to participate, began traveling across the United States in the service of the Central Park Commission, looking for traces of animals to base his models on. In the meantime, his assistants were furnishing a studio for him in the Central Park Arsenal and began constructing the first giant dinosaur models according to his design.

Most New Yorkers, naturally, were enchanted by the promise of a museum whose catacombs were occupied by these fantastical creatures. But just like the inventor Alfred Beach at this time, Hawkins had unwittingly made an enemy of William Tweed, who recognized the popular appeal of this project without seeing a way to derive profit for himself. He assigned a few of his men to infiltrate the Central Park Commission and look for a way to block the museum. Worse, he arranged for a group of vandals to break into Hawkins's studio and smash the dinosaur models to pieces. He succeeded. Disgusted by New York and its unsavory methods, Hawkins abandoned the project and returned to London.

But the broken dinosaur models still exist—buried at Mount St. Vincent in Central Park. They were tossed into the pit that had already been excavated in anticipation of

PALAEOZOIC    MUSEUM.
SHOWING THE REHABILITATED FORMS OF ANCIENT ANIMAL LIFE IN AMERICA
NOW BEING CONSTRUCTED IN CENTRAL PARK.

*Figure 23.7A  The proposed Paleozoic Museum in Central Park*

*Figure 23.7B Because of the collection's massive weight, the American Museum of Natural History stores its dinosaur bones in the basement*

the diorama, and after the hole was filled in with soil, the dinosaur pieces disappeared from public memory and were never uncovered. When the subway was constructed along the western edge of Central Park, none of the remnants were found.

Yet New York was to have its dinosaurs after all. The site of the city's first scientific museum was relocated shortly after Hawkins's departure a few blocks further north, to a rugged patch of land at Central Park West and 79th Street, which was then mainly occupied by goats and pigs. Here, President Ulysses Grant laid the cornerstone of the American Museum of Natural History in 1874. The first building of the Victorian-style museum was opened in 1877.

Today the museum is a complex of 24 structures, which are only partially open to the public. On the basement and attic levels are the museum's largest storage areas, filled with scientific curiosities: mummies, bats, gems, alcohol-filled vats with the body parts of rare animals, and millions of other artifacts. The dinosaur room, where many of the fossilized bones are stored, lies along an underground passage on the museum's lowest level. Because of the weight of the bones, the well-organized brightly lit room has to rest directly on bedrock. Perhaps, just like these fossils, Hawkins's models will someday be excavated and reassembled from bits and pieces, creating a curiosity in their own right.

*Figure 24.1  The formerly secret wine cellar at "21" stores a valuable collection of spirits*

# CHAPTER TWENTY-FOUR

# Breweries, Speakeasies, and Wine Cellars

A history of New York's underground would be incomplete without its rich legacy of gastronomic enterprises, since so much subterranean space was once occupied by breweries and speakeasies, not to mention the multitude of clubs, bars, and restaurants occupying the city's basements to this day.

Breweries once flourished in New York. By 1860, the city was home to 40 such establishments, and in 1900 there were almost 50 in Brooklyn alone. One section in Williamsburg between Bushwick Place and Lorimer Street, where 12 breweries had settled by 1880, was designated "Brewers' Row." Next to Philadelphia and Milwaukee, New York was considered the American capital of beer until the steep rents forced out most brewers in the first half of the twentieth century. The beer was often stored in the cool cellars beneath the buildings, some of which, such as the former Nassau Brewery on Franklin Street, still retain a few original features even as the buildings have been converted to other functions.

One of the best known was the F&M Schaefer Brewing Company. The Schaefers had introduced New York to German lager beer in 1842. From their original location at Broadway and 18th Street, the Schaefers moved to Fourth Avenue and 50th Street in 1849, where the Waldorf-Astoria stands today. When construction began on the new Grand Central Terminal, the Schaefer Brewery complained that the excavations for the tracks were damaging its foundation, and after winning a lawsuit, they relocated their facilities to a massive new building constructed on Kent Street along the Williamsburg waterfront. During Prohibition from 1920 to 1933, the brewery kept itself afloat with the sale of nonalcoholic beer, soda, and ice.

In 1976, after having gradually transferred most of its production to Allentown, Pennsylvania, the Schaefer Brewery closed its doors on Kent Street, leaving behind an incredibly fascinating ruin. Some 20 years later, while it had become dangerously decrepit, it had also turned into a seemingly inexhaustible playground, with many

*Figure 24.2 A washroom inside the basement of the recently demolished Schaefer Brewery in Williamsburg*

underground passageways, huge kettles, hidden ladders and stairways, and a flooded sub-basement, where old machinery was staining the water red with rust. Along with piles of old beer bottles, many remnants of the building's functions were left behind, and until it was demolished in 2001, it was a formidable relic of Brooklyn's rich brewing history.

Whereas breweries suffered during Prohibition, the speakeasies profited all the more. "21" was the most famous club illegally serving alcohol in New York. It opened in 1920 under the name "Red Head" in Greenwich Village and changed its address three times before settling permanently inside a residential house on 52nd Street. A doorman ensured that neither the police nor any troublemakers were admitted, since the main business of what to all appearances was just a restaurant

*Figure 24.3 In the cellar of the former Nassau Brewery on Franklin Street in Brooklyn*

was the illegal alcohol trade. For years this operation went smoothly, until a large raid in 1930 temporarily put the club out of business. Yet the owners of "21" were not easily defeated. They assigned a group of architects and engineers to the task of designing a better way to hide the booze.

The club underwent an unusual reconstruction. The owners built fake walls and doors, new stairs, and secret shafts. One closet had a hidden mechanism, activated by touching a metal coat hanger to a particular hook in the wall, which resulted in a door popping open to reveal a cache of wine. With the touch of a button, the shelves behind the bar would slide backward. The bottles then dropped down a hidden chute and shattered against rocks.

Whenever the doorman saw a cop approach the door to "21," he would set off an alarm and all alcohol would magically disappear. On one particular night in June 1932, the alarm was sounded, and shortly afterward a group of investigators entered the club. For 12 hours they searched the entire building—all the closets, shelves, and storage rooms—even the basement. The strong smell left by the shattered bottles drove them crazy, yet they could find nothing. The club was obviously

*Figure 24.4  A private dining room adjacent to the wine cellar in "21"*

just another fancy restaurant. And yet 2,000 cases of the finest wines, including vintages from the 1880s, were stored on the premises.

So where was the hiding place? There was a small niche in the basement that was obviously used as a storage area. Dried goods were piled on the floor, and hams dangled from the ceiling. What the investigators couldn't suspect was that the rear wall of the niche was actually a secret door, since at a weight of two and a half tons, it gave all the appearances of being a solid wall, even if someone banged against it. It could be opened only when a very thin rod was inserted into a tiny hole, where it unlatched a lock mechanism. The room this door opened into was the basement of the adjoining house and was thus technically not part of the club. This way the owners hoped to protect their employees from having to lie to the authorities.

The heavy door opened not only into the wine cellar but into an elegant room in the rear, equipped with booths and designed for private parties. One regular guest during Prohibition was Mayor Jimmy Walker, who did not like to be interrupted while he enjoyed a good glass of wine and retreated down there whenever the police showed up. His favorite booth is still inside one of the private rooms.

After Prohibition was lifted in 1933, "21" continued as a distinguished restaurant, attracting numerous famous diners, from Ernest Hemingway to Frank Sinatra, Dorothy Parker to Humphrey Bogart. To this day the restaurant's wines are kept

CHAPTER TWENTY-FIVE

# The Crypts Beneath
# New York's First Cathedral

Among the most historic, and yet least accessible, underground spaces in New York are the burial catacombs that still rest beneath some of the city's churches. Many New Yorkers will have heard of the Marble Cemetery between Second Avenue and the Bowery, which consists entirely of underground chambers; the vaults below St. John the Divine, accessible to the public on Halloween for guided "crypt crawls"; and the tomb of Peter Stuyvesant, New York's famous seventeenth-century governor, beneath St. Mark's-in-the-Bouwerie. Yet, New York, unlike so many other cosmopolitan cities, has been reluctant to display its architecture of death. More typically, it seals the doors to its tombs and lets entire burial vaults slide into oblivion, thus occassionally spooking its contractors with surprising discoveries.

The construction of a subway section in the early twentieth century, for instance, resulted in uncovering a tomb below an old church on Bedford Street, where about 8,000 people had been interred before it was sealed and forgotten in the mid-1800s. When a contractor broke through into one of the subdivided chambers, finding several coffins, even the church authorities were surprised. The remains in the 20 vaults inside the tomb, which were connected by underground passages, had to be relocated to proceed with the construction under Seventh Avenue.

In 1965, Con Edison workers sinking a shaft at the northeast corner of Washington Square came across a curved rock surface and assumed it was part of an abandoned tunnel. When they broke through, they found a sealed vault with 25 skeletons inside, which they quickly covered up again. These and similar episodes lead one to wonder how many other burial vaults still rest unknown in New York's underground.

There is one crypt, at least, that is about to enter the world of the living. Although the catacombs below the city's first cathedral, Old St. Patrick's on Mott Street, have been closed to the public, the space has been well-preserved. While

*Figure 25.2 When it opened in 1815, the original St. Patrick's Cathedral on Mott and Prince streets was the city's largest building of worship*

the original cathedral building burned down in the nineteenth century, its basement was untouched by the fire and the church's subsequent restoration. This is fortunate, as nearly the entire cellar below the church is occupied by crypts filled with the remains of both bishops and families whose descendants live on.

When the cathedral's cornerstone was laid in 1809, the plot of land at Mott and Prince streets was considerably north of the city's center in an area lush with meadows and wooded hills. Named after Ireland's patron saint and primarily attracting Irish Catholics, St. Patrick's Cathedral opened in 1815 as the largest building of worship in the city. Soon it found itself a target of mob riots. Starting in the 1830s, anti-immigrant sentiments led to increasing violence by the nativists, who felt particularly threatened by the numbers of Irish Catholics flooding into the city. To protect itself, the church erected a wall, and by stationing armed Irish defenders on its premises, it helped deter a nativist mob in 1836.

In 1842, John Hughes became the fourth bishop of New York and was soon nicknamed "Dagger John," not only for the dagger-like cross that accompanied

*Figure 25.3 The vault of "Honest" John Kelly, who reorganized Tammany Hall
after the reign of the notoriously corrupt William Tweed*

his signature, but for his fierce defense of the Irish community. In the mid-nineteenth century, crime and poverty were rampant, ethnic and nativist gangs fought bloody battles in the Five Points area, and orphans and prostitutes lined the streets. Alcohol, drugs, and diseases had infiltrated the tenements. Bishop Hughes sought to get the Irish off the streets and re-educate them, innovating a number of social programs—including a Catholic school system—while continuing the battle against anti-Catholic attacks.

The gang wars had escalated dangerously by 1844, and one day a massive nativist mob began marching up from City Hall with torches, intent on burning the cathedral to the ground. In response, Dagger John armed the members of the Ancient Order of Hibernians, an Irish defense group, and stationed the sharpshooters on the church walls. He had also warned Mayor James Harper that the city would be devastated by violence should harm come to a single Catholic. Thanks to his interference, the mob disbanded before the cathedral could be damaged. His efforts had a noticeable impact, although pitched battles between ethnic gangs took years to subside.

Having withstood these threats, the church was almost entirely destroyed by an accidental fire in 1866, and had to be rebuilt. In 1879, the seat of New York's Archdiocese moved to the newly constructed St. Patrick's Cathedral on Fifth Avenue, while the old cathedral became a parish church. This meant that all subsequent bishops would be interred in the new cathedral's crypt beneath the altar rather than in the vaults on Mott Street. The remains of Archbishop Hughes, originally entombed at Old St. Patrick's, were moved to the new crypt, as were those of Pierre Toussaint, a former Haitian slave who had helped raise money for the old cathedral's construction and whose canonization is currently underway.

*Figure 25.4 A private vault is embellished with a tile ceiling by Rafael Guastavino*

As the current rector of Old Saint Pat's, Father Thomas Kallumady is interested in making its historic crypt accessible to the public. To be buried here, a prospective vault owner had to have influential ties to the church and the Irish community, since space was extremely limited, and this in turn means that at least some of the deceased are likely to have played a role in some of the city's more notable historic events. This heritage is something Father Kallumady would like to explore and preserve.

The space itself has undergone many changes. The original architecture of the crypt did not entirely survive renovations. It has been painted white and no longer sits beneath an arched ceiling. Yet the tombs are intact, filling three aisles with 12 vaults to each row. The most recent burial, of the cathedral's pastor from 1954 to 1970, is in a tomb in the rear, and one unoccupied tomb awaits a final casket. Nearly all of the other spaces, however, had been sealed by the mid-nineteenth century. Among the more familiar names carved into the stone plates are Bishop John Connolly; the Tammany Hall leader "Honest" John Kelly; the restaurateur Francis Delmonico; the country's first papal countess, Annie Leary; and the family tomb of the Civil War photographer Mathew Brady.

One tomb lies separate and was clearly added after the others. It is the only one with a real door and is furnished with ornate lamps and a stand for a prayer book. Here, there is a hidden gem: the green-tiled ceiling was designed by Rafael Guastavino, who also created the vaults at the Oyster Bar and the original City Hall Station. Finding his work here, in a small chamber few are ever likely to see, was a nice surprise.

Ars Subterranea, which is working with Father Kallumady to present the crypt to the public as of the writing of this book, discovered a secret passage in this space. There had been rumors of a private pedestrian tunnel from the cathedral basement to the rectory on Mulberry Street, which was built to provide a safe exit in case any calamity befell the church. Accompanied by Father Kallumady, Ars Subterranea members were able to poke around the rectory basement until the sealed door to the tunnel was found. Although this tunnel below Mulberry Street seems to at least partially be filled in, it was nonetheless exciting to discover such a passageway in the crowded Manhattan underground.

*Figure 26.1  An abandoned track leading to one of the Canal Street station platforms*

CHAPTER TWENTY-SIX

# The Attraction of the Underground

On a warm summer evening some years ago, I met up with a few friends from California who were trying to decide how to round off their visit to New York. One of these was John Law, a veteran urban adventurer from the now disbanded San Francisco Suicide Club, who was always up for an unusual exploration. We decided that we would take a walk along the waterfront of the East River, toward a hatch behind an abandoned building that looked like a promising entry into the underground.

The waterfront was desolate, but as we approached, we saw that the metal doors of the hatch were flung open, revealing a brightly lit room at the bottom of a short ladder. No one seemed to be around and we cautiously stepped inside. The room opened to another staircase leading much deeper into the ground; some of us began to descend, while a few of our visitors still lingered near the entrance, wondering whether to continue. We were a few flights down the stairs when the railing suddenly began to vibrate. Far beneath us there was an ominous rumbling sound, quickly getting louder, accompanied by a strong gust of air. Had a gate opened somewhere, letting in a surge of water from the East River? Alert, we hesitated, until we heard a familiar drone. A subway train was passing below us at high speed.

Now our guests were intrigued and began to follow. Nine stories below the hatch we came onto a small platform between two train tracks. Apparently we were at an emergency exit at the mouth of an underwater tunnel. It was pleasantly cool down here and smelled of moist earth. A sudden shrill alarm went off, startling us; then we realized that it was just a warning of an approaching train. A minute later the train rushed past us with a blast of air that nearly threw us off balance.

Aside from the brightly lit staircase and the occasional blue tunnel light, it was very dark. At the end of the platform stood a shack with a flat roof. Behind it was a wall, each of its sides bordering on the two tracks. Next to one of the rail beds was a ladder leading to the roof of the shack, and we decided to climb up and stay a while. Behind us, running up the wall between the tracks, was another ladder to a small, mysterious shaft in the

221

ceiling, which seemed as if it might open to still other passages. One of our friends, eager to investigate, began to climb the decrepit rungs, while two others decided to light up cigars and relax on our cozy roof. Then we heard another train, only this one was slowing down as it approached.

Immediately the cigars were put out and we threw ourselves flat on the roof, while our friend on the ladder just stayed there, probably in the hopes that the train would pass. Unfortunately it didn't. It was one of the small yellow garbage trains, and it stopped right at our platform. Above us we heard a creaking. Our friend had broken one of the rungs and was now dangling awkwardly against the wall, trying to keep still. Only a few feet below us, the MTA workers were getting off; there were loud shuffling sounds as they picked up heavy bags from inside the shack and tossed them onto the train, cursing all the while. The bright light from the train projected the silhouettes of the men onto the tunnel walls, casting our friend above us in the spotlight. We would be discovered any moment. Couldn't they smell the smoke from the damn cigars?

The workers were shouting at each other to hurry. The next subway train would come any moment along the same tracks. Then, incredibly, they got back on, and the

*Figure 26.2  The emergency exit of a subway tunnel below Central Park has recently been alarmed*

train slowly began moving away. We didn't wait for the next round. We jumped off the shack and just as we began to climb the stairs back to the surface, we heard the approach of another subway at top speed: the yellow train had left just in time.

That experience was a pretty good instance of what I consider having a great time in New York, and for some reason there are others who share this opinion. The elements of adventure and discovery are only part of it. Similar to watching a live surgery, it affords a glimpse into something so vital to our existence that is nonetheless kept hidden from public view. Centuries ago, the dissection of bodies was prohibited; now this great organism keeping the city running beneath its surface is something whose inner workings we are not supposed to see. Yet coming across men at work inside the mysterious deep strata in this way is a rare unmediated experience of visceral New York.

Anyone who has begun to pay attention to the city's subterranean labyrinths, who notices manhole covers, peers into shafts and wonders about those illuminated exits in the subway tunnels, might be getting a taste of the inexhaustible scope of New York's underground realms. Although for most people the leap from simple curiosity to an actual exploration is a large one, it is a means of transforming the anonymous city into a personal space. Taking a risk in accessing particular underground areas tends to help form a meaningful bond to the location. "The fascination for me is from really seeing what the environment I move through each day rests upon," says John Law. "When you start looking underneath the surface you see entire worlds, some of which are currently in use and some of which are completely dormant—almost the archaeological remnants of past cities. You can see the skin sloughed off. It's so organic, because the city is growing on levels and levels of prior lives and infrastructures."

People who explore the underground of their own accord are fairly rare in New York, but they come from vastly different backgrounds, and often their interest is fueled by working in professions that expose them to the subterranean city. Whether they are transit workers, cops, or sandhogs, they may still enjoy an extracurricular walk along an intriguing set of tracks. Much more rare are subterranean explorers who descend solely out of passion for the underground. These adventurers take great risks to find and document hidden places, to speculate about the former functions of obsolete machinery and delight in the discovery of any quirky signs or artifacts.

Urban explorers in New York are a relatively small group who tend to know each other and foster each other's interests. As in the graffiti world, there is also an element of competition. Because the discovery of a new and spectacular place in New York's underground is such a rare occurrence, an explorer might guard the location carefully both to avoid attention from the authorities and to prevent a future collision with underground tourists. Sometimes this leads to an "I'll show you mine if you show me yours" exchange, with the understanding that secret entry points will remain secret,

*Figure 26.3  Chris Beauchamp descends into one of the steep drops of the Croton Aqueduct*

and usually this works out well. By now, however, there are quite a few exploration and photography Web sites on formerly hidden locations, and the solitude that still reigns in many of these places comes almost as a surprise.

The fact that only a few people venture into New York's underbelly is something that Christos Pathiakis particularly appreciates. He has explored the subway tunnels for many years and developed ghostly photos of the abandoned City Hall Station on small copper plates. Likewise, the photographer Joseph Anastasio—a former graffiti writer with an extensive knowledge of the city's subway tunnels—tries to capture unusual images down here, which also serve as a record of his infiltrations. "Part of tagging was about being able to say, 'I was here,'" he says. "With the photographs I could do the same and show them off to others as well." His familiarity with subway history makes Joe a good match for any rail buff, with the additional experience of actually having been in underground locations most people have never heard of.

Aside from the veteran explorers, there are also a number of younger kids who simply jump off the subway platforms and take a hike along the tracks out of sheer curiosity, such as an explorer who goes by the name Quest, who contacted me to share his excitement about scoping out an abandoned station in Manhattan. "I must say that the rush I get when just running through from track to track is enough to make me feel I'm at home in the subway," he says. "All I know is that I'm hooked now."

*Figure 26.4 The exit line for Ars Subterranea's exhibition on underground New York
inside the Atlantic Avenue Tunnel*

Such unauthorized excursions are frowned upon by most of the rail buffs who
proliferate the many online message boards dedicated to New York's subway system,
exchanging intricate details about train models, route changes, and signal malfunctions.
The more fanatic of these are nicknamed foamers, because speaking about the subway
is said to get them so excited that they foam at the mouth. The front window in the first
train car, from which the tracks can be seen ahead, is the foamer window.

With all this interest in the New York underground, it is unfortunate that
there are so few places suitable for public visits and that, unlike in cities such as
Paris, Berlin, and Vienna, there are no regular tours of interesting subterranean sites.
Visiting the Transit Museum in Brooklyn, partaking in one of the rare forays into
the Atlantic Avenue Tunnel, and dining at the Oyster Bar at Grand Central just about
complete the sightseeing activities of underground New York. The abandoned

*Figure 26.5  For just a moment, the author emerges back into the light of day*

City Hall Station, which many people are clamoring to visit, would make a great addition to this list, and hopefully a day will come when terrorist concerns are less critical and New York will again take pride in its subterranean heritage.

Although I would not repeat such a journey in this current climate, our guests from San Francisco will remember their adventure down the subway hatch more vividly than any visit to the top of the Empire State Building. Anyone who would like to gain an authentic sense of New York has to take its subterranean regions into account just as much as the structures above. Exploring the underground means taking a journey into what anchors this city in history. Regardless of the reasons for going there, the world beneath New York is inexhaustible, and will always continue to attract the curious.

# Bibliography

GENERAL REFERENCE

Alexander, Charles. "Time to Repair and Restore; Neglected Streets and Sewers, plus Aged Bridges and Byways, Hinder Growth." *Time*, April 27, 1981.

Berger, Meyer. *Meyer Berger's New York*. New York: Random House, 1960.

Bilger, Burkhard. "The Crumbling Skyline." *The New Yorker*, December 4, 2000.

*Brooklyn Daily Eagle*, "Transit Development for Greater New York," June 1, 1902.

Burrows, Edwin G. and Wallace, Mike. *Gotham*. New York: Oxford University Press, 1999.

Caro, Robert A. *The Power Broker, Robert Moses and the Fall of New York*. New York: Alfred A. Knopf, 1974.

Chartock, David S. "Regional Boom to Continue in 2001." *New York Construction News*, January 2001.

Chen, David W. "Be It Ever So Low, the Basement Is Often Home." *New York Times*, February 25, 2004.

Choi, Sunghoon. "A Potpourri of Tunnels in New York City." *Korean-American Scientific Engineers Association*, March 1, 2002.

Daley, Robert. *The World Beneath the City*. Philadelphia: Lippincott, 1959.

Davidson, Marshall B. *New York. A Pictorial History*. New York: Charles Scribner's Sons, 1977.

Dukart, James R. "New Ways to Go Underground." *Utility Business*, September 2000.

Dunlap, David W. "Old York." *New York Times*, December 20, 2000.

Dunning, Jennifer. "A Downside-Up Look at How New York Ticks." *New York Times*, May 29, 1981.

Gies, Joseph. *Adventure Underground*. Garden City: Doubleday and Company, 1962.

Goodwin, Maud Wilder, et al. *Historic New York*. New York: G.P. Putnam's Sons, 1899.

Granick, Harry. *Underneath New York*. New York: Fordham University Press, 1947.

Guttenplan, D.D. "Invisible Metropolis Bustles Beneath City." *Newsday*, October 1, 1989.

Homberger, Eric. *The Historical Atlas of New York City*. New York: Henry Holt & Co., 1994.

Homberger, Eric. *Scenes from the Life of a City*. New Haven: Yale University Press, 1994.

Hornung, Clarence P. *The Way It Was. New York 1850–1890*. New York: Schocken Books, 1977.

Huxtable, Ada Louise. *Classic New York*. Garden City: Doubleday and Company, 1964.

Jackson, Donald Dale. "It Takes a Sixth Sense to Operate Under the Streets of New York." *Smithsonian Magazine*, August 1987.

Jackson, Kenneth, ed. *The Encyclopedia of New York City*. New Haven: Yale University Press, 1995.

Jarosz, Stanley and Patel, Mahendra. "New York-Style Rehab Program." *Public Works*, June 1, 1999.

Jones, Pamela. *Under the City Streets*. New York: Henry Holt & Co., 1978.

Kandell, Jonathan. "Boss." *Smithsonian Magazine*, February 2002.

Kaufman, Leslie and Flynn, Kevin. "New York's Homeless, Back Out in the Open." *New York Times*, October 2, 2002.

Knox, Thomas W. *Underground, or: Life Below the Surface*. Hartford: The J. B. Burr Publishing Company, 1874.

Lavine, David. *Under the City*. Garden City: Doubleday and Company, 1967.

McCain, Mark. "Foundations: Learning to Cope 3ith Myriad Subterranean Surprises." *New York Times*, August 14, 1998.

McShane, Larry. "Under the Big Apple: 'There's an Entire World.'" *Associated Press*, August 27, 1989.

Morris, Lloyd. *Incredible New York*. New York: Random House, 1951.

*New York Times*, "With the Moles of This Great Metropolis," May 14, 1905.

*New York Times*, "Tunnel Workers Victims of Poetry Habit," April 7, 1907.

*New York Times*, "In the Underground City of New York," July 21, 1929.

Porter, Henry. "Eyes That Can't Stand the Light." *The Guardian*, March 8, 1996.

Smith, Donald. "Underworlds; Lair of Evil? More Like Pipes, Cables." *Orange County Register*, June 19, 1995.

Stern, Robert A.M., Gilmartin, Gregory, and Massengale, John. *New York 1900*. New York: Rizzoli, 1995.

Swan, Christopher. "A Mole's Eye View of New York City." *Christian Science Monitor*, September 4, 1980.

Treadwell, David and Tumulty, Karen. "A Conspiracy of Engineering and Decay; Old Infrastructure Leads to Freak Accidents in N.Y." *Los Angeles Times*, October 9, 1989.

Willensky, Elliot and White, Norval. *AIA Guide to New York City*. New York: Macmillan, 1978.

*The WPA Guide to New York City: The Federal Writers Project Guide to 1930s New York*. New York: The New Press, 1992.

## A CITY BUILT ON TREACHEROUS ROCK

Allen, Michael O. "Ground Zero Yields Burial Ground Relics." *Daily News*, November 15, 2001.

Barry, Dan. "Manhattan Past, Queens Present: City Hall Artifacts Are Returned From Obscurity" *New York Times*, July 16, 2001.

Binder, David. "Geology Map Due for Manhattan." *New York Times*, July 16, 1961.

Buder, Leonard. "Hidden Stream at School Site Causes $100,000 Delay in Work." *New York Times*, October 14, 1963.

Buttenwieser, Ann L. *Manhattan Water-Bound*. Syracuse: Syracuse University Press, 1999.

Cantwell, Anne-Marie and Wall, Diana diZerega. *Unearthing Gotham: The Archaeology of New York City*. New Haven: Yale University Press, 2001.

Chernow, Ron. "The Silent Springs of Manhattan." *New York Times*, March 6, 1977.

Fairfield, Hannah. "City Lore; The Rock That Gives New York Its Face" *New York Times*, September 24, 2000.

Gasnick, Jack. "Dig He Must, and City Yields Old Treasures." *New York Times*, January 16, 1972.

Gopnik, Adam. "Underfoot." *The New Yorker*, February 4, 2002.

Hobbs, William Herbert. *The Configuration of the Rock Floor of Greater New York*. Washington: Government Printing Office, 1905.

Horenstein, Sidney. "Big Apple Tusks." *Natural History*, March 1989.

Ingrassia, Robert. "$21M Plan Mired in Woe; Researchers, Feds Wrangle Over African Burial Ground." *Daily News*, February 5, 2001.

Koeppel, Gerard. "Digging the Urban Past: A Subterranean Panorama." *New York Observer*, January 21, 2002.

Lorber, Claudia. "Digging Up Our Urban Past" *New York Times*, April 12, 1981.

Luo, Michael. "Another Burial for 400 Colonial-Era Blacks." *New York Times*, October 2, 2003.

Mather, William W. *Natural History of New York. Part IV: Geology*. Albany: Carroll & Cook, 1843.

*New York Times*, "Sources of Great Danger. Underground Streams as Breeders of Contagion," January 17, 1892.

*New York Times*, "Buried Streams Trouble New York Builders," February 10, 1907.

*New York Times*, "Quicksand Made Safe for Building," January 12, 1959.

Reeds, Chester A. *The Geology of New York City and Vicinity*. New York: The American Museum of Natural History, 1925.

Suggs, Robert C. *The Archaeology of New York*. New York: Thomas Y. Crowell, 1966.

## STRUGGLING FOR FRESH WATER

Barnard, Charles. "The New Croton Aqueduct." *Century Magazine*, December 1889.

Burke, Jack. "New York Water; Water Tunnel No. 3." *Mining Journal*, March 1996.

Chiles, James R. "Remember, Jimmy, Stay Away from the Bottom of the Shaft!" *Smithsonian Magazine*, July 1994.

Collins, Glenn: "In City's History, a Glass Half Full; Unearthed Archives Reveal Artistry of Water Supply." *New York Times*, January 8, 2001.

Dwyer, Jim. "TA Sinks Pretense of Caring." *Newsday*, December 5, 1989.

*Engineering and Mining Journal*, "Modern Mine Practice in the Construction of a 20-Mile Aqueduct," June 8, 1929.

Fifield, Adam. "The Underground Men." *New York Times*, January 12, 2003.

Garrett, Rodney. "New York Shafts; Maintenance and Rehabilitation of New York City's Water Distribution System." *Mining Journal*, May 1994.

Gill, John Freeman. "Decrepit Water Main Could Blow Anytime Right Under Fifth." *New York Observer*, May 28, 2001.

Grann, David. "City of Water." *The New Yorker*, September 1, 2003.

Hu, Winnie. "Mayor Goes 550 Feet Below to Note Start of Tunnel Construction." *New York Times*, October 9, 2003.

Koeppel, Gerard T. *Water for Gotham*. Princeton: Princeton University Press, 2000.

Lehman College. "Jerome Park Reservoir and the History of the Croton Waterworks." http://lcw. lehman.edu/lehman/preservationreport/history.html.

Martinez, Jose: "Memorial to Honor 23 Killed Digging City Water Tunnel." *Daily News*, November 1, 2000.

McFadden, Robert D. "Water System; The Marvelous Monster." *New York Times*, January 18, 1988.

Mittelbach, Margaret and Crewdson, Michael. "Water Works." *Brooklyn Bridge*, November 1995.

*The New York Beacon*, "New York City Agrees to Filter Croton Drinking Water System," June 4, 1998.

*New York Times*, "Mayor Holes Out Aqueduct Tunnel," January 13, 1914.

*New York Times*, "In 100-Mile Tunnel Hike," January 19, 1914.

*New York Times*, "Found the Aqueduct Wet," January 20, 1914.

Purnick, Joyce. "New York Has Reason to Pour $2.7 Billion into a Hole in the Ground." *New York Times*, April 26, 1981.

Raftery, Tom and Rose, Derek. "Water Main Break Floods Bronx Subway." *Daily News*, November 14, 2001.

Revkin, Andrew C. "21st Century Plumbing for a Leaky Old Aqueduct." *New York Times*, March 12, 2002.

Stohr, Kate. "Water." *Gotham Gazette*, December 8, 2003.

Wasserman, Joanne. "Aqueduct Alarm Is All Wet, Rudy Says." *Daily News*, November 4, 2000.

Wilkinson, Alec, "Going Downstairs." *Doubletake*, Summer 2001.

Winter, Greg and Broad, William J. "Added Security for Dams, Reservoirs and Aqueducts." *New York Times*, September 26, 2001.

Witherspoon, Roger. "Region's Water System Due for Upgrade." *The Journal News*, December 21, 2003.

## IN THE WAKE OF THE CROTON MAID

Bahrampour, Tara. "Now in an Old Gatehouse, Art, Not Water, Will Flow." *New York Times*, February 25, 2001.

Bryant, Nelson. "City's Water System: A Wonder of Engineering." *New York Times*, December 14, 1986.

*Daily News*, "Walk History's Path," March 11, 2001.

Duncan, Steve. "The Hidden Flow of History. The Path of the Aqueduct in Today's New York." www.undercity.org.

FitzSimons, Neal. *The Reminiscences of John B. Jervis, Engineer of the Old Croton*. Syracuse: Syracuse University Press, 1971.

Gray, Christopher. "The High Bridge Water Tower; Fire-Damaged Landmark to Get $900,000 Repairs." *New York Times*, October 9, 1988.

Kugel, Seth. "Neighborhood Report: Highbridge; Trying to Make a Historic Crossing More than a Relic." *New York Times*, March 24, 2002.

Moss, Jordan. "Architect Unearths Rich Reservoir History." *Norwood News*, September 24–October 7, 1998.

*New York Times*, "Huge Steel Arch in High Bridge Plan," April 20, 1924.

Richards, T. Addison. "The Croton Aqueduct." *Harper's New Monthly Magazine*, December 1860.

Rideing, William H. "Croton Water." *Scribners Monthly*, June 1877.

Siegal, Nina: "Plugging a Hole in the Reservoir of Memory." *New York Times*, May 7, 2000.

Ultan, Lloyd. "Poe's Bronx Horror." *Riverdale Review*, October 25, 2001.
Wolfer, Sondra. "High Hopes for Bridge." *Daily News*, July 14, 2002.


## AN ALLIGATOR MARKS THE SEWERS

Birch, Eugenie L. "Planning in a World City: New York and Its Communities." *Journal of the American Planning Association*, September 22, 1996.
Buffa, Denise. "Parks Big: Sewer Life Would Be Gator-Aid." *New York Post*, June 20, 2001.
Elliott, Andrea. "Sewage Spill Exposed a Lingering City Problem." *New York Times*, August 28, 2003.
Goldman, Joanne Abel. *Building New York's Sewers: Developing Mechanisms of Urban Management.* West Lafayette: Purdue University Press, 1997.
Kaplan, Fred. "This NYC Urban Legend Has Teeth." *Boston Globe*, June 22, 2001.
Kilgannon, Corey. "A Parkgoer in Alligator Skin? Call 911." *New York Times*, April 29, 2003.
Mann, Roy. *Rivers in the City*. New York: Praeger Publishers, 1973.
Markowitz, Michael. "The Sewer System." *Gotham Gazette*, October 10, 2003.
Mitra, Nirmal. "Engineer Helps Rebuild New York City." *India Abroad*, January 12, 1996.
*New York Times*, "Automobiling in Sewers," May 18, 1902.
*New York Times*, "Twenty Passers-By Hurt in Gas Explosion," September 10, 1919.
*New York Times*, "Alligator Found in Uptown Sewer," February 10, 1935.
*New York Times*, "Sewer Blasts Dim Area in Brooklyn," November 25, 1947.
Perry, Nancy J. and Berlin, Rosalind Klein. "The Economy: Good News About Infrastructure." *Fortune*, April 10, 1989.
Pyle, Richard. "DEP Says: Send Gator Back to the Sewer." *Associated Press*, June 19, 2001.
Shipler, David. "A Vast Underground Network Supports Life of the City." *New York Times*, December 19, 1968.
Siegel, Joel. "The Sewer Alligator." *Daily News*, June 18, 2002.
Stewart, Barbara. "Dressed for the Park, in Alligator Skin." *New York Times*, June 21, 2001.
Treaster, Joseph B. "Nearly Two Miles of Sewer Blasts Injure 11 Persons in South Bronx." *New York Times*, March 23, 1978.
Wieman, Clark. "Downsizing Infrastructure." *Technology Review*, May 15, 1996.


## A MAZE OF PIPES BENEATH THE STREETS

Bevelhymer, Carl. "Steam." *Gotham Gazette*, November 11, 2003.
Blair, Jason. "Near Ground Zero, Street Surgery Starts with a Shovel." *New York Times*, March 14, 2002.
*Brooklyn Daily Eagle*, "Pneumatic Mail Tubes," November 12, 1896.
*Brooklyn Daily Eagle*, "Pneumatic Tube Service," October 1, 1902.
Conan, Neal. "Talk About Steam Engines." *Morning Edition*, NPR, December 31, 1993.
*Concrete Pumping Magazine*, "New York City Record," Fall 2003.
Crawford, Linda. "City Woos New Tech." *Gotham Gazette*, January 8, 2001.
Duffus, R. L. "Metal Roots That Feed the Living City." *New York Times*, April 13, 1930.
Dukart, James R. "New Ways to Go Underground." *Utility Business*, September 2000.
Feuer, Alan. "Three Transformers to Bring New Power to Ground Zero." *New York Times*, November 9, 2003.
*Fifty Years of New York Steam Service*. New York: New York Steam Corporation, 1932.
Hemphill, Christina. "Electricity." *Gotham Gazette*, December 8, 2003.
Jacobs, Charles M. *A General Report Upon the Initiation and Construction of the Tunnel Under the East River*. New York: 1894.
*The Manufacturer and Builder*, "Underground Telegraph Lines," June 1876.
*The Manufacturer and Builder*, "Labyrinth of Pipes Under New York," May, 1880.
*The Manufacturer and Builder*, "The Blizzard and the Telegraph," April 1888.
M'Vey, G. H. P. "Laying a 24-Inch Gas Main Across the Harlem River." *Scientific American*, September 15, 1900.
McDonald, Michael. "Con Ed's High Stakes Game of Phone Tag." *Crain's New York Business*, September 11, 2000.
*New York Times*, "Met Death in the Wires: Horrifying Spectacle on a Telegraph Pole," October 12, 1889.
Perlow, Dustin. "Old Timers Recall Blizzard of '88." *Daily Star*, March 11, 1915.

Pogrebin, Robin. "Underground Mail Road." *New York Times*, May 7, 2001.

Saulny, Susan. "Two Are Hurt as Electrical Explosion Blows Manhole Cover in Air in Midtown." *New York Times*, March 13, 2001.

Slackman, Michael. "Neither Snow nor Rain, but G.O.P." *New York Times*, October 13, 2003.

Stohr, Kate. "Studying How to Avoid Blackouts." *Gotham Gazette*, August 3, 2003.

Sullivan, Robert. "Dig It." *New York Times*, May 12, 2002.

Taylor, Tess. "Whoosh." *The New Yorker*, November 17, 2003.

*Time Out New York*, "How New York Works," July 19–26, 2001.

Vescovi, James. "Underground Mailroad." *Inc Magazine*, June 15, 1994.

Virasami, Bryan. "Manhole Cover Erupts, Injures 5 Cops." *Newsday*, February 15, 2000.

*Voice of New York*, "Giuliani Announces Initiative to Transform Unused Water Main into Conduit" April 26, 2000.

Williams, Sam. "Natural Gas." *Gotham Gazette*, October 10, 2003.

Wilson, Greg: "That Sinking Feeling." *Daily News*, July 31, 2001.

Wofsey, Michael. "Back to the Future." *Wired*, May 1994.

Wren, Christopher S. "All That Digging in Streets Has Interior Motive." *New York Times*, July 27, 1973.

Young, Shawn and Berman, Dennis K. "Trade Center Attack Highlights Problem in Telecom Sector's Legacy of Monopoly." *Wall Street Journal*, October 19, 2001.

## THE SECRET SUBWAY OF ALFRED BEACH

Beach, Alfred Ely. "The Pneumatic Tunnel Under Broadway, NY." *Scientific American*, March 5, 1870.

Bobrick, Benson. *Labyrinths of Iron*. New York: Newsweek, 1981

*Illustrated Description of the Broadway Underground Railway*. New York: The Beach Pneumatic Transit Company, 1872.

Maeder, Jay. "Notes from the Underground: The Subway 1904." *Daily News*, December 31, 1999.

*New York Times*, "Destructive Fire in Sky-Scrapers," December 5, 1898.

*New York Times*, "Rogers, Peet & Co's Building," December 5, 1898.

*New York Times*, "First Subway 40 Years Ago," February 4, 1912.

*New York Times*, "Visit Old Pneumatic Tunnel," February 9, 1912.

*New York Times*, "Old Tunnel Company to Fight Subways," February 22, 1912.

*Public Service Record*, "Broadway Subway Now Open," September, 1917.

Weeks, Helen C. "What a Bore!" *The Youth's Companion*, February 2, 1871.

## WELCOME TO THE SUBWAY CRUSH

Byrnes, Nanette. "Special Report: The Future of New York: Rebuilding the City Underground." *Business Week*, October 22, 2001.

Cho, Aileen. "Engineers Are Digging Deep to Rebuild New York's Subways." *Engineering News-Record*, April 12, 2004.

Cudahy, Brian J. *Malbone Street Wreck*. New York: Fordham University Press, 1999.

Cuza, Bobby. "Design of Second Avenue Subway Approved." *Newsday*, November 27, 2001.

Danziger, Jeff. "Digging Up the Facts About New York's Subway System." *Christian Science Monitor*, September 7, 1993.

Donohue, Pete. "Subway & Bus Use Highest in Decades." *Daily News*, March 24, 2002.

Donohue, Pete. "Second Avenue? Big Subway Dig Looms." *Daily News*, May 12, 2003.

*Engineering News-Record*, "Mole Chews Up a Mile of Rock," March 19, 1981.

Fischler, Stan. *The Subway: A Trip Through Time on New York's Rapid Transit*. New York: H&M Productions, 1997.

Fried, Joseph P. "Untangling Knots in the Subway." *New York Times*, February 3, 2000.

Glaser, Julius. "The Design of Subways." *Public Service Record*, October/November 1918.

Hood, Clifton. *722 Miles; The Building of the Subways*. Baltimore: Johns Hopkins University Press, 1995.

Katz, Celeste and Saul, Michael. "Mayor: 7 Train Comes First." *Daily News*, January 30, 2002.

Kennedy, Randy. "This Straphanger Rode with Class." *New York Times*, June 26, 2001.

Kennedy, Randy. "An Old Rivalry, A Quiet Continuance." *New York Times*, August 21, 2001.

Kennedy, Randy. "Tunnel to Nowhere, Except Maybe the Future." *New York Times*, October 21, 2003.

Lavis, F. "The New York Rapid Transit Railway Extensions." *Engineering News*, November 12, 1914.

*Mining Journal, World Tunnelling*, "Manhattan Subway Plans Advance," December 1, 2001.

*The New York Subway*. New York: Interborough Rapid Transit, 1904.

*New York Times*, "Man Killed in Subway," November 4, 1904.

*New York Times*, "Things Seen and Heard Along the Underground," October 28, 1904.

*New York Times*, "Worker Shot Skyward from Under River Bed," March 28, 1905.

*New York Times*, "Subway Clear to Brooklyn," March 2, 1907.

*New York Times*, "Scores Killed, Many Hurt on B.R.T.," November 2, 1918.

Payne, Christopher. *New York's Forgotten Substations*. New York: Princeton Architectural Press, 2002.

Quinby, E. J. "Minnie Was a Lady." *Railroad*, February 1956.

Rainie, Harrison. "Tunnels to Nowhere." *Washington Monthly*, March 1, 1986.

Rayman, Graham and Brown, Joshua. "City Wants $2B MTA Land Swap." *Newsday*, February 26, 2004.

Sanchez, Ray. "2nd Avenue Line: Fact or Fiction?." *Newsday*, December 6, 2001.

Sargent, Greg. "The Line That Time Forgot." *New York Magazine*, April 5, 2004.

Schoener, Allon. "Times Square Subway Station: Follow the Red Lights to Utter Confusion." *Herald Tribune*, May 9, 1965.

*The Second Avenue Subway Line . . . the Line That Almost Never Was*. New York: New York City Transit Authority, 1972.

Stengren, Bernard. "Shuttle Is Short, Except in History." *New York Times*, April 22, 1964.

Tierney, John. "Substitute for a Subway on Second Avenue: Free Enterprise." *New York Times*, December 5, 2000.

Young, Robin. "Beneath the City That Never Sleeps." *The Times (UK)*, May 2, 1992.

## GHOST STATIONS

Brennan, Joseph. "Abandoned Stations." www.columbia.edu/~brennan/abandoned/.

Daley, Robert. "Elegant but Abandoned IRT City Hall Stop Proposed as Museum." *New York Times*, January 16, 1965.

Duggan, Dennis. "Magic Under 18th Street." *Newsday*, February 8, 2002.

Fischler, Stan. *The Subway: A Trip Through Time on New York's Rapid Transit*. New York: H&M Productions, 1997.

Kennedy, Randy. "Next Stop, 'Twilight Zone' (aka 76th St. Station)." *New York Times*, January 21, 2003.

*New York Times*, "Buses Take Over Williamsburg Run," December 6, 1948.

*Record and Guide*, "How the Subway Platforms Were Extended," March 4, 1911.

Toth, Jennifer. *The Mole People: Life in the Tunnels Beneath New York City*. Chicago: Chicago Review Press, 1993.

Ward, Nathan. "Underworld." *Architecture*, April 1, 2001.

## SILENT TUNNELS

Andelman, David A. "Tunnel Project, Five Years Old, Won't Be Used." *New York Times*, October 11, 1980.

Burks, Edward C. "Coming: Light at End of the 63d St. Tunnel." *New York Times*, September 24, 1976.

Dolman, Joseph. "Queens Gets Tunnel for Crushed Masses." *Newsday*, November 28, 2000.

Dougherty, Peter. *Tracks of the New York City Subway*. New York, 2001.

Martin, Douglas. "Under New York, the Tracks That Time Forgot." *New York Times*, November 17, 1996.

Prial, Frank J. "63rd St. Tube Put into East River." *New York Times*, August 30, 1971.

Saltonstall, Dave. "TA Repair Work Sending System into a Tailspin." *Daily News*, March 26, 2001.

Saulny, Susan. "Another Tunnel Offers Breathing Room for E and F Trains." *New York Times*, November 28, 2000.

## MOVING TRAINS BELOW THE HUDSON

*Brooklyn Daily Eagle*, "Shocking. Fatal Disaster in the Hudson River Tunnel," July 21, 1880.

*Brooklyn Daily Eagle*, "The Hudson River Tunnel Project," May 28, 1887.

Burr, S.D.V. *Tunneling Under the Hudson River.* New York: John Wiley and Sons, 1885.
Fitzherbert, Anthony: "William G. McAdoo and the Hudson Tubes." *Electric Railroaders Association,* June 1964.
*The Manufacturer and Builder,* "The Hudson River Tunnel Disaster," August 1880.
*New York Times,* "Science in Tunnel Building," October 1, 1880.
*Scientific American,* "The Cortlandt Street Tunnels and Terminal Building, New York," January 26, 1907.
*Tunnels and Tunnelling International,* "PATH Prepares for a New Era," September 1, 2002.
Wildman, Edward. "The Wonders of Underground New York." *The World To-Day,* 1908.


## THE RISE AND FALL OF PENN STATION

*Associated Press,* "Disaster Lurks for Rail Commuters," July 7, 2001.
Bagli, Charles V. "Deal Revives Delayed Plan for Train Hub." *New York Times,* October 8, 2002.
Chartock, David. "East End Concourse: Meeting the Challenges of Underground Construction." *New York Construction News,* November 2001.
Collins, Glenn. "40 Years After Wreckage, Bits of Old Penn Station." *New York Times,* October 28, 2003.
Diehl, Lorraine B. *The Late, Great Pennsylvania Station.* New York: Viking Penguin, 1987.
Fetherston, Drew. "The Manhattan Connection: Workers in a Perilous Craft Create a Web of East River Tunnels to Speed LIRR Commuters." *Newsday,* April 17, 1998.
McGinty, Jo Craven. "Amtrak: The Price of Safety." *Newsday,* December 21, 2001.
Murphy, Dean E. "Penn Station Needs Millions for Repairs." *New York Times,* December 19, 2000.
Murphy, Dean E. "State Faults Amtrak for Neglect of Tunnels." *New York Times,* August 23, 2001.
*New York Times,* "Truck Buried Near Waldorf," December 15, 1906.
*New York Times,* "Must Open the Streets to Finish Penna. Tunnel," February 1, 1907.
Sadik-Khan, Janette. "New York Forum About Penn Station." *Newsday,* September 22, 1993.


## THE MYSTERIES OF GRAND CENTRAL

Belle, John and Leighton, Maxinne R. *Grand Central: Gateway to a Million Lives.* New York: W.W. Norton & Company, Inc., 1999.
Bernard, Walter. "The World's Greatest Railway Terminal." *Scientific American,* June 17, 1911.
Dillon, David: "Grand Stand." *The Dallas Morning News,* November 22, 1998.
Duffus, R. L. "Metal Roost That Feed the Living City." *New York Times,* April 13, 1930.
Duggan, Dennis. "Paving a Way? They Can't Shrug It Off." *Newsday,* February 18, 1997.
Ellis, Elaine A. "Moving Homeless from Grand Central Tunnels." *Gannett News Service,* August 4, 1991.
Frisman, Paul. "The Snowmen Melt." *The Connecticut Law Tribune,* June 30, 1997.
Goldberger, Paul. "Grand Central Basks in a Burst of Morning Light." *New York Times,* June 3, 1990.
Gray, Christopher. "A Look Down at the Rail Tunnels Below Park Ave." *New York Times,* November 25, 2001.
Grondahl, Paul. "A Chronicle of 4 Years Under Grand Central." *The Times Union,* October 18, 2001.
Hart, Jeffrey. "Architecture Simply Grand. The Restoration of Grand Central Terminal." *National Review,* November 9, 1998.
Henican, Ellis. "The Asbestos Crisis—MTA Workers on Asbestos Firm What a Mess." *Newsday,* August 10, 1993.
*The Journal News,* "Discovering the Secrets of Grand Central Terminal," September 9, 2001.
*Metropolitan Transportation Authority,* "East Side Access: The Long Island Rail Road Grand Central Connection," Spring 2000.
Middleton, William D. *Grand Central: The World's Greatest Railway Terminal.* San Marino: Golden West Books, 1977.
Murphy, William. "Ruling Against Snowmen." *Newsday,* June 24, 1997.
*New York Times,* "Constructing a Great Modern Railway Terminal," August 16, 1908.
*New York Times,* "Pipe Gallery Built Without Authority," March 30, 1909.
*New York Times,* "Grand Central Zone Boasts Many Connected Buildings," September 14, 1930.
Rogoff, David. "The Steinway Tunnels." *Electric Railroads,* April 1960.
S., Tina and Bolnick, Jamie Pastor. *Living at the Edge of the World.* New York: St. Martin's Press. 2000.

Safer, Morley. "Grand Central; $200 Million Housecleaning Turns Grand Central Station into a Spotless, Born-Again Terminal." CBS News, July 13, 1999.

Saltzman, Steven and Senft, Bret. "Grand Central Terminal." *Metropolis*, September 1991.

Schaer, Sidney C. "Grand Central Plan on Track/LIRR Extension to Terminal Has Gained Important Ground." *Newsday*, February 19, 2000.

Schlichting, Kurt C. *Grand Central Terminal*. Baltimore: John Hopkins University Press, 2001.

*Scientific American*, "A Great Subterranean Railway Junction," November 19, 1910.

Shackleton, Robert. "Fifty-Three Tracks Abreast in the Heart of New York." *Technical World*, February 1905.

Steinberg, Jacques. "Coaxing Grand Central's Homeless into the Light." *New York Times*, March 17, 1992.

*Tunnels & Tunnelling International*, "Preparing for a Piece of East Side Access Action," December 1, 2002.

Valenti, John: "Next Stop for the LIRR: Grand Central by 2011." *Newsday*, January 18, 2002.

## AN OVERVIEW

Anderson, Steve. "Lower Manhattan Expressway." www.nycroads.com/roads/lower-manhattan

Anderson, Susan Heller and Dunlap, David W. "Big Name and Short Road." *New York Times*, August 25, 1986.

*Crain's*, "Port Authority Gives Tunnel Go-Ahead." November 2003.

Cross Harbor Freight Movement Project. "Cross Harbor Study Freight Movement." www.crossharborstudy.com.

Jamieson, Wendell. "Riding the Bounding Rails." *New York Times*, March 2, 2003.

*Newsday*, "Link LI to Mainland with a Tunnel Under the Sound," June 2, 2001.

Robin, Joshua. "Report: Build New Hudson Tunnel." *Newsday*, December 8, 2003.

Valenti, John. "An 'Act' That Affects Us All." *Newsday*, November 19, 2003.

Wilson, Linda J. "Cross Harbor Project Could Bring 3,000–7,000 New Jobs." *Western Queens Gazette*, October 29, 2003.

## THE LOST TUNNEL OF ATLANTIC AVENUE

Baumgartner, Henry: "The Lost Tunnel of Brooklyn." *Mechanical Engineering Magazine*, 1998.

*Brooklyn Daily Eagle*, "Accident at the Tunnel," August 19, 1844.

*Brooklyn Daily Eagle*, "Opening of the Tunnel," December 5, 1844.

*Brooklyn Daily Eagle*, "Steam on Atlantic Street," December 29, 1858.

*Brooklyn Daily Eagle*, "That Tunnel," May 22, 1866.

*Brooklyn Daily Eagle*, "Tunnel Road: An Underground Railway for Atlantic Avenue." April 20, 1886.

*Brooklyn Daily Eagle*, "Atlantic Avenue Tunnel," May 31, 1896.

*Brooklyn Daily Eagle*, "Tunnel Mystery Probers Reach Wall in Sewer." July 28, 1936.

Diamond, Bob and Ricciardi, Vincent R. *The Atlantic Avenue Tunnel*. New York: Brooklyn Historic Railway Association.

English, Merle. "Underground Rail Tunnel Raised to Landmark Status" *Newsday*, July 27, 1989.

English, Merle. "Historic Tunnel Links the Past with the Future." *Newsday*, October 27, 1991.

Fulbright, Newton H. "Brooklyn's Mystery Tunnel Is 'Discovered' All Over Again." http://arrts-arrchives.com/tunnel.html

*New York Times*, "Old Tunnel Eludes Police Explorers," July 29, 1936.

Otterman, Sharon and Ach, Michael. "Beneath the Avenue, a Tunnel of History." *Newsday*, July 16, 1995.

Weir, Richard. "Half a Mile Long, and Nearly Forgotten." *New York Times*, April 4, 1999.

## THE FREEDOM TUNNEL

Buttenwieser, Ann L. *Manhattan Water-Bound*. Syracuse: Syracuse University Press, 1999.

Dunlap, David W. "Turning a View into a Point of View." *New York Times*, August 29, 2002.

Fowler, Geoffrey A. "Living in the Shadows." *U.S. News & World Report*, September 11, 2000.

Gottlieb, Martin. "Rail Fan Finds Rusting Dream on West Side." *New York Times*, January 16, 1984.

Lombardi, Frank. "Track Park Plan Derailed." *Daily News*, December 2001.

Maeder, Jay. "Big Things. Men at Work, July 1981." *Daily News*, October 2001.

McCann, Colum. "People Say We Eat Rats, but Food Is the Least Damn Problem in New York." *The Observer*, July 16, 1995.

Morton, Margaret. *The Tunnel*. New Haven: Yale University Press, 1995.

Polner, Robert. "Help! No Pets Allowed." *Newsday*, July 16, 1996.

Sicha, Choire. "Hanging Garden of Babble-On." *New York Observer*, November 17, 2003.

Singer, Mark. "My Seven Years with the Mole Men." *The Guardian*, March 2, 2001.

*The Toronto Star*, "Getting Off the Streets," February 17, 2002.

*West Side Improvement*. New York: New York Central, 1934.

Wilson, Calvin. "Shedding Light on Life in the Dark." *St. Louis Post-Dispatch*, April 26, 2001.

## PLAYGROUNDS OF THE UNDERWORLD

Asbury, Herbert. *The Gangs of New York*. New York: Thunder's Mouth Press, 1998.

*Brooklyn Daily Eagle*, "The Arrest of John Allen," Octobber 19, 1868.

*Brooklyn Daily Eagle*, "Thawed Out Successfully," November 25, 1898.

*Brooklyn Daily Eagle*, "Killed in a Saloon by Detective Doyle," April 12, 1899.

Fifield, Adam. "The Knockoff Squad." *New York Times*, June 23, 2002.

Hall, Bruce Edward. "Chinatown." *American Heritage*, April 1999.

Hall, Bruce Edward. "The Forbidden City." *Time Out New York*, March 8, 2001.

*Harper's New Monthly Magazine*, "New York Harbor Police," October 1872.

Kinkead, Gwen. *Chinatown — A Portrait of a Closed Society*. New York: HarperCollins, 1992.

Lee, Denny. "Years of the Dragons." *New York Times*, May 11, 2003.

*New York Times*, "Bold Attempt to Rob a Bank," March 26, 1861.

*New York Times*, "Byrnes Says He Has a Clue." April 26, 1891.

*New York Times*, "Caught in Tunnel Leading to a Bank," January 7, 1910.

*New York Times*, "Find Painter's Body in East Side Tunnel," January 8, 1910.

*New York Times*, "Tunnel in Street Mystifies Police," September 28, 1924.

*New York Times*, "Hobo Club in Park Wiped Out in Raid," December 15, 1930.

Young, James C. "South Street Whispers of Shanghaiing." *New York Times*, March 21, 1925.

## TUNNELS FOR THE MASSES

*Bergen Record*, "Transit Agency Shuts Crime-Ridden Tunnel, Concedes the Action Was Overdue," March 24, 1991.

Fine, Marshall. "Shhh . . . These Are the Secret Passages." *The Journal News*, June 2001.

Fowler, Glenn. "Rockefeller Center Growing Down." *New York Times*, March 21, 1971.

Henican, Ellis. "6th Avenue's Dark Tunnel of Crime." *Newsday*, March 24, 1991.

Hoffman, Jan. "Subway Rape Victim Tries to Prove Agency Was at Fault." *New York Times*, August 31, 1994.

Kugel, Seth. "2 Elevators for 2 Riderships at Nearby Subway Station." *New York Times*, January 7, 2001.

Kurtz, Josh. "A Subway Passageway Just for the Courageous." *New York Times*, August 12, 1991.

*New York Times*, "Excavation Gazing Put on a New Plane." November 11, 1938.

## THE TUNNELS OF SEAVIEW HOSPITAL

Gray, Christopher. "Seaview Hospital; A TB Patients' Haven Now Afflicted with Neglect." *New York Times*, July 16, 1989.

Iverem, Esther. "Rescued WPA Works Go on Exhibit." *Newsday*, October 5, 1993.

Lerner, Barron. "Once Upon a Time, a Plague Was Vanquished." *New York Times*, October 14, 2003.

O'Grady, Jim. "Walls That Talk, Vividly, of Healing Mercies." *New York Times*, May 21, 2000.

*New York Times*, "Seaview Transformed into Geriatrics Hospital," June 4, 1973.

*New York Voice Inc./Harlem USA*, "City to Seek Developer for Senior Citizen Housing on Sea View Hospital Campus," September 10, 2003.

Shelby, Joyce. "City's on Track for Morgue in S.I." *Daily News*, July 29, 1996.

## THE LABYRINTH BELOW COLUMBIA UNIVERSITY

Adie, Tristin. "New York Forum About Columbia — Suppressing the Spirit of '68." *Newsday*, March 3, 1993.

Columbia Student Solidarity Network. "What Lies Beneath the Real Columbia Underground." New York. 2000.

Homans, Charlie. "Urbanities. Forbidden Tunnels Guard CU History." *Columbia Spectator*, February 27, 2004.

Lane, Earl. "Hiroshima. The Manhattan Project Scientists. *Newsday*, July 17, 1995.

*New York Times*, "Columbia's New Location: Bloomingdale Grounds Now Owned by the College," September 26, 1894.

Schreiber, Michael R. and Rodriguez-Nava, Gabriel. "Under Columbia: Where the Ivy Doesn't Grow." *NYC24*, February 21, 2003.

Scott, Michael. "Hacking the Material World." *Wired*, July-August 1993.

Siegfried, Tom. "Atomic Bomb Altered World History." *The London Free Press*, January 2, 1999.

Sydell, Laura; Wertheimer, Linda, and Adams, Noah. "Columbia '68 Anniversary." *All Things Considered*, NPR, April 23, 1998.


## THE GRAFFITI OF DEAD SOLDIERS

Ben-Yehuda, Ayala. "City Awaits Draft Proposal for Transfer of Fort Totten." *Whitestone Times*, December 4, 2003.

Brouwer, Norman. "Defending New York City's Eastern Gateway: A History of Fort Totten on Willets Point." *Bayside Historical Society*, 1996.

Duggan, Dennis. "Victory in Long Battle Over Fort Totten." *Newsday*, April 27, 2004.

English, Merle. "At Fort, Battle Over a Building." *Newsday*, September 14, 2002.

English, Merle. "Land of Dreams. Groups Add Vision to Plan for Surplus Property at Fort Totten." *Newsday*, October 20, 2003.

Ferris, Marc. "The Battle of Fort Tilden. Should Nature or Military History Take Priority?" *Newsday*, July 7, 2000.

Horsley, Carter. "The Present Intrudes on an Old Fort's Reverie." *New York Times*, March 21, 1976.


## NEW YORK'S LARGEST FOUNDATION

Blair, Jayson. "In an Urban Underbelly, Hidden Views of Terror's Toll." *New York Times*, October 14, 2001.

Blair, Jayson. "Near Ground Zero, Street Surgery Starts with a Shovel." *New York Times*, March 14, 2002.

Chivers, C.J. "Looting Is Reported in Center's Tomblike Mall." *New York Times*, September 21, 2001.

Cockfield, Errol A. "Subways Around WTC Tested for Safety." *Newsday*, September 15, 2001.

Dewan, Shaila K. "Twin Peaks Make a Vertical World of Their Own." *New York Times*, February 27, 2001.

Donohue, Pete. "More of Subway on Track." *Daily News*, September 19, 2001.

Donohue, Pete. "E Train to Stop at WTC Soon." *Daily News*, January 24, 2002.

Donohue Pete and Saul, Michael. "$2M WTC Hub to Soar in Sunshine." *Daily News*, January 23, 2004.

Dwyer, Jim. "Below Ground Zero, Silver and Gold." *New York Times*, November 1, 2001.

Ellison, Michael. "A Dream in Ruins." *The Guardian*, January 22, 2002.

Fink, Jason. "WTC Station Back to Being PATH's Busiest." *The Jersey Journal*, February 13, 2004.

Flynn, Kevin. "Rescuers See Hope in Trip into the Dark of a Tunnel." *New York Times*, September 18, 2001.

Frank, Al. "P.A. Looks at Options for New Downtown Terminal." *Star Ledger*, October 25, 2001.

Gearty, Robert. "WTC Find Seals Drug Bust." *Daily News*, January 17, 2002.

Gilbert, Pat R. "Massive Repairs Needed Before Trains Run Again." *Bergen Record*, November 15, 2001.

Gillespie, Angus Kress. *Twin Towers*. New York: Rutgers University Press, 1999.

Gittrich, Greg and Donohue, Pete. "$1M-a-Day Fix for WTC Subway." *Daily News*, January 16, 2002.

Gittrich, Greg, Zambito, Thomas, and Standora, Leo. "Cache of Gold Found at WTC." *Daily News*, October 31, 2001.

Glanz, James. "From 70s Relic, a Possible PATH Station." *New York Times*, November 13, 2001.

Glanz, James. "Below Rubble, a Tour of Still-Burning Hell." *New York Times*, November 15, 2001.

Glanz, James and Lipton, Eric. "The Excavation: Planning, Precision and Pain." *New York Times*, September 27, 2001.

Glanz, James and Lipton, Eric. "In the Pit, Dark Relics and Last Obstacles." *New York Times*, January 13, 2002.

Iglauer, Edith. "The Biggest Foundation." *The New Yorker*, November 4, 1972.

Johnson, Kirk and Bagli, Charles V. "Architects, Planners and Residents Wonder How to Fill the Hole in the City." *New York Times*, September 26, 2001.

Kennedy, Randy. "Subway by Trade Center to Take Years to Rebuild." *New York Times*, September 28, 2001.

Kennedy, Randy. "Same Old Subway Stop. Just Don't Go Up the Steps." *New York Times*, February 5, 2002.

Kennedy, Randy. "A Subway Interrupted Awaits Its Imminent Resurgence." *New York Times*, May 21, 2002.

Landau, Sarah Bradford and Condit, Carl W. *Rise of the New York Skyscraper.* New York: PUB, 1996.

Lipton, Eric. "Nuts and Bolts (and Water) Challenge 9/11 Shrine." *New York Times*, January 24, 2004.

McKibben, Bill. "New York's True Heart." *New York Times*, October 7, 2001.

*Mobile Communications Report*, "Verizon Struggles to Restore NY Switching Center to Service," September 17, 2001.

*New York Times*, "Office Building Here to Be Largest Yet," August 5, 1925.

Overbye, Dennis. "Engineers Tackle Havoc Underground." *New York Times*, September 18, 2001.

Overbye, Dennis. "Under the Towers, Ruin and Resilience." *New York Times*, October 9, 2001.

Rayman, Graham. "Water Leaks at Ground Zero Worse than They Thought." *Newsday*, February 7, 2002.

Rogers, Josh. "Beginning to Put Downtown Plans in Place." *Downtown Express*, April 9, 2003.

Rybczynski, Witold. "The Future of Up." *New York Times*, December 9, 2001.

Sabbagh, Karl. *Skyscraper; The Making of a Building.* New York: Penguin, 1990.

Seabrook, John. "The Tower Builder." *The New Yorker*, November 10, 2001.

Stewart, William R. "Underground New York." *Technical World*, February 1905.

Tamaro, George J. "World Trade Center 'Bathtub': From Genesis to Armageddon." *The Bridge*, Spring 2002.

Wyatt, Edward. "Designs Unveiled for Transit Hub at Ground Zero." *New York Times*, November 13, 2002.

Zupan, Jeffrey M. "Transportation and Lower Manhattan: Where Do We Go From Here?" *Gotham Gazette*, May 5, 2003.

## UNUSUAL FOUNDATIONS

*Brooklyn Daily Eagle*, "Completion of the Brooklyn Anchorage," August 26, 1875.

*Brooklyn Daily Eagle*, "The New York and Brooklyn Approaches," July 14, 1877.

*Brooklyn Daily Eagle*, "Caisson Launch Successful," May 15, 1897.

Cohen, David S. "Locked in Realm of Monstrous Terror." *South China Morning Post*, March 16, 1997.

Conaut, William. "The Brooklyn Bridge." *Harper's Monthly*, May 1883.

Dunlap, David W. "When Expansion Leads to Inner Space." *New York Times*, May 5, 2002.

Fetherston, Drew. "Gateway to a Century: The Magnificent Brooklyn Bridge Becomes the Last Great Work of an Age." *Newsday*, March 15, 1998.

Graves, Neil. "Library's History Is a Real Page Turner." *New York Post*, December 27, 1999.

Holder, J. B. "The American Museum of Natural History." *Century Magazine*, August 1882.

Martin, Douglas. "Behind Dinosaurs, It's the Mounting Team's Game." *New York Times*, June 26, 1995.

Nash, Deborah. "Secret London: Triassic Park; Dinosaurs at Crystal Palace." *The Independent Sunday*, December 7, 2003.

*New York Times*, "Big Water Main Bursts: Pipe in 42nd Street Breaks but Causes Little Damage." November 15, 1900.

Polner, Rob. "Eviction of the 'Bridge People' Leaving Shadow World." *Newsday*, June 9, 1994.

Post, Nadine M. "Walking on Books in an Urban Park." *Engineering News Record*, February 23, 1989.

Preston, Douglas J. "The Museums That Almost Were; Natural History Museums in New York City." *Natural History*, March 1984.

Preston, Douglas J. *Dinosaurs in the Attic.* New York: St. Martin's Press, 1986.

Richardson, Lynda. "The Man with the X-Ray Eyes." *New York Times*, April 2, 2000.

Rouse, Dana. "Digital Fossils: Archiving the American Museum of Natural History." *Photo District News*, March 1, 2003.

Schneider, Daniel B. "F.Y.I." *New York Times*, January 10, 1999.

Wallach, Amei. "You Are There; Go Hunting for the Hidden History of a Museum That's Been Telling Us Who We Are for 125 Years." *Newsday*, January 20, 1995.

Weber, Bruce. "E. L. Doctorow's New York." *New York Times*, July 5, 1994.

## BREWERIES, SPEAKEASIES, AND WINE CELLARS

Anderson, Will. *Breweries of Brooklyn.* Croton Falls: Will Anderson, 1976.

Brick, Michael. "At a Venerable Manhattan Haunt, Ghosts of a Speakeasy Past." *New York Times*, December 6, 2003.

*Brooklyn Daily Eagle*, "Lager Beer. Where and How the Beverage Is Made," August 2, 1870.

*Brooklyn Daily Eagle*, "Lager Beer. A Trip Through the Breweries of Williamsburgh," August 12, 1875.

*Brooklyn Daily Eagle*, "A Day's Journey Through a Great Brooklyn Brewery," November 9, 1884.

Fabricant, Florence. "Restaurant Wine 'Cellars': Some Untraditional Locations." *New York Times*, November 28, 1984.

Hall, Carol. "Neighbors Unite: Unusual Pair Develop Unused Site." *Newsday*, August 30, 1989.

Jankowksi, Ben. "The Bushwick Pilsners: A Look at Hoppier Days." *Brewing Techniques*, January/February 1994.

Kriendler, H. Peter and Jeffers, H. Paul. *"21."* Dallas: Taylor Publishing, 1999.

Rayman, Graham. "Big Dealings in Brooklyn Plan: Pact at Old Brewery Site Taps Controversy." *Newsday*, November 9, 2002.

Schneider, Daniel B. "F.Y.I." *New York Times*, March 29, 1998.

## THE CRYPTS BENEATH NEW YORK'S FIRST CATHEDRAL

*Brooklyn Daily Eagle*, "The Late Bishop's Crypt," October 22, 1893.

Carthy, Mother Mary Peter. *Old St. Patrick's. New York's First Cathedral.* New York: United States Catholic Historical Society, 1947.

Concannon, Ken. "'Dagger John' and the 'Gangs of New York.'" *Catholic Herald*, March 20, 2003.

Cook, Leland. *St. Patrick's Cathedral.* New York: Quick Fox, 1979.

Montgomery, Paul L. "Skeletons Found in Washington Square." *New York Times*, August 2, 1965.

*New York Times*, "Tombs Under the City," August 2, 1896.

*New York Times*, "Veritable Catacombs in the Heart of a Populous New York Block," December 3, 1905.

*New York Times*, "Ancient Cemeteries Dug Up in Subways," June 11, 1916.

Sheedy, Robert. "The First Saint Patrick's Cathedral." *Greenwich Village Gazette*, Vol. 6, No. 26, 2001.

Stern, William J. "How Dagger John Saved New York's Irish." *City Journal*, Spring 1997.

Zielbauer, Paul. "Marble Walls, Roomy, but No Place to Live." *New York Times*, May 23, 2000.

# Index

# Image Credits

[Abbreviation: JS = Julia Solis]

## 1. INTRODUCTION
1.1 Chris Beauchamp
1.2 JS
1.3 JS
1.4 Harry Haller
1.5 JS

## 2. A CITY BUILT ON TREACHEROUS ROCK
2.1 JS
2.2 From: Hobbs, William Herbert. *The Configuration of the Rock Floor of Greater New York*. Washington: Government Printing Office, 1905.
2.3 From: Reeds, Chester A. *The Geology of New York City and Vicinity*. New York: The American Museum of Natural History, 1925.
2.4 Author's Collection
2.5 Mike Donnelly

## 3. STRUGGLING FOR FRESH WATER
3.1 JS
3.2 Author's Collection
3.3 Author's Collection
3.4 From: Barnard, Charles. "The New Croton Aqueduct." *Century Magazine*, December 1889.
3.5 From: Barnard, Charles. "The New Croton Aqueduct." *Century Magazine*, December 1889.
3.6 From: Barnard, Charles. "The New Croton Aqueduct." *Century Magazine*, December 1889.
3.7 From: Barnard, Charles. "The New Croton Aqueduct." *Century Magazine*, December 1889.
3.8 From: *Engineering and Mining Journal*, "Modern Mine Practice in the Construction of a 20-Mile Aqueduct," June 8, 1929.
3.9 JS

## 4. IN THE WAKE OF THE CROTON MAID
4.1 JS
4.2 JS
4.3 Rob Schmitt
4.4 Chris Beauchamp
4.5 Author's Collection
4.6 JS

9.4 JS
9.5 JS

## 10. SILENT TUNNELS

10.1 JS
10.2 Harry Haller
10.3 JS
10.4 JS
10.5 JS
10.6 JS
10.7 JS
10.8 JS

## 11. MOVING TRAINS BELOW THE HUDSON

11.1 Author's Collection
11.2 From: Wildman, Edward. "The Wonders of Underground New York." *The World To-Day*, 1908.
11.3 Author's Collection
11.4 From: *Scientific American*, "The Cortlandt Street Tunnels and Terminal Building, New York," January 26, 1907.
11.5 Author's Collection
11.6 From: *Scientific American*, "The Cortlandt Street Tunnels and Terminal Building, New York," January 26, 1907.

## 12. THE RISE AND FALL OF PENN STATION

12.1 Author's Collection
12.2 Postcard, Author's Collection
12.3 Author's Collection
12.4 JS
12.5 JS

## 13. THE MYSTERIES OF GRAND CENTRAL

13.1 Postcard, Author's Collection
13.2 JS
13.3 Author's Collection
13.4 From: Shackleton, Robert. "Fifty-Three Tracks Abreast in the Heart of New York." *Technical World*, February 1905.
13.5 Postcard, Author's Collection
13.6 JS
13.7 JS
13.8 Author's Collection
13.9 JS
13.10 From: *Scientific American*, "A Great Subterranean Railway Junction," November 19, 1910.
13.11 JS
13.12 JS
13.13 JS
13.14 JS
13.15 JS

## 14. AN OVERVIEW

14.1 JS
14.2 JS
14.3 JS

**15.    THE LOST TUNNEL OF ATLANTIC AVENUE**

15.1    Courtesy of Bob Diamond
15.2    JS
15.3    Courtesy of Bob Diamond
15.4    JS
15.5    Courtesy of Bob Diamond
15.6    JS
15.7    JS


**16.    THE FREEDOM TUNNEL**

16.1    JS
16.2    JS
16.3    JS
16.4    JS
16.5    JS
16.6    Harry Haller


**17.    PLAYGROUNDS OF THE UNDERWORLD**

17.1    From: *Harper's New Monthly Magazine*, "New York Harbor Police," October 1872.
17.2    JS
17.3    JS


**18.    TUNNELS FOR THE MASSES**

18.1    JS
18.2    JS
18.3    JS


**19.    THE TUNNELS OF SEAVIEW HOSPITAL**

19.1    JS
19.2    JS
19.3    JS
19.4    JS
19.5    JS


**20.    THE LABYRINTH BELOW COLUMBIA UNIVERSITY**

20.1    JS
20.2    Author's Collection
20.3    JS
20.4    JS
20.5    JS
20.6    JS


**21.    THE GRAFFITI OF DEAD SOLDIERS**

21.1    JS
21.1B    JS
21.2    JS
21.3    JS
21.4    JS
21.5    JS

## 22.    NEW YORK'S LARGEST FOUNDATION

22.1    JS
22.2    George J. Tamaro, Courtesy of Mueser Rutledge Consulting Engineers
22.3    Author's Collection
22.4    George J. Tamaro, Courtesy of Mueser Rutledge Consulting Engineers
22.5    George J. Tamaro, Courtesy of Mueser Rutledge Consulting Engineers
22.6    George J. Tamaro, Courtesy of Mueser Rutledge Consulting Engineers
22.7    JS
22.8    JS
22.9    George J. Tamaro, Courtesy of Mueser Rutledge Consulting Engineers

## 23.    UNUSUAL FOUNDATIONS

23.1    Courtesy of Creative Time
23.2    JS
23.3    From: *Harper's Weekly*, December 17, 1870.
23.4    JS
23.5    Joseph Anastasio
23.6    JS
23.7A   Courtesy of Carl Mehling
23.7B   JS

## 24.    BREWERIES, SPEAKEASIES, AND WINE CELLARS

24.1    JS
24.2    JS
24.3    JS
24.4    JS
24.5    JS
24.6    JS

## 25.    THE CRYPTS BENEATH NEW YORK'S FIRST CATHEDRAL

25.1    JS
25.2    Collection of Anne Polster
25.3    JS
25.4    JS

## 26.    THE ATTRACTION OF THE UNDERGROUND

26.1    Harry Haller
26.2    JS
26.3    JS
26.4    Chris Beauchamp
26.5    Chris Beauchamp

## COLOR

In order of placement
Bryan Papciak
Chris Beauchamp
JS
JS
Chris Beauchamp
JS
Aaron Benoy
JS

JS
JS

JS
JS
JS
Harry Haller
JS
JS
JS
JS
JS
JS
JS

JS
Chris Beauchamp
Chris Beauchamp
 JS
JS
JS
JS
Harry Haller
JS
Harry Haller

JS
JS
Steve Duncan
JS
JS
JS
JS
George J. Tamaro, Courtesy of Mueser Rutledge Consulting Engineers
Courtesy of Creative Time
JS
JS

# About the Author

Julia Solis began publishing stories and documentations of ruined spaces after receiving a B.A. in philosophy in 1990. As the proprietress of Dark Passage and an officer of the Madagascar Institute, she founded the creative preservation group Ars Subterranea in 2002, with the object of staging events in New York's derelict and underground locations. Also in 2002, she published the German edition of *New York Underground* (Christoph Links, Berlin) and subsequently received a fellowship from the New York Foundation for the Arts for this edition of the book.